CISTERCIAN STUDIES SERIES: NUMBE

David N. Bell

A Cloud of Witnesses:

An Introduction to the Development of Christian Doctrine to AD 500
Second, revised edition

This is a copy of what is arguably the best known of all icons, painted by the Russian monk Andrei Rublev (*c.* 1360/70–*c.* 1430) in about 1411. The original was made for the Cathedral of the Dormition of the Virgin in Vladimir, but is now preserved in the Tretyakov Gallery in Moscow. The subject is the three angels who appeared to Abraham at Mamre and told him that Sarah, his wife, would have a son (Gen 18:1-16). Sarah, with good reason, did not believe it, but God's will could not be forestalled, and in due course she gave birth to Isaac. The three angels were widely regarded by patristic writers as an Old Testament symbol and anticipation of the Christian Trinity, though some—a minority—saw only the angel at the head of the table (here in a dark robe) as a symbol of God the Son, accompanied by two other angels. Almost all later representations of the scene were influenced by Rublev's magnificent icon.

THE HOSPITALITY OF ABRAHAM

Icon by Eileen McGuckin
Location: The Icon Studio, New York
Photo: Eileen McGuckin

CISTERCIAN STUDIES SERIES: NUMBER TWO-HUNDRED EIGHTEEN

A CLOUD OF WITNESSES:

AN INTRODUCTION TO THE DEVELOPMENT OF CHRISTIAN DOCTRINE TO AD 500

Second, revised edition

by

David N. Bell

Cistercian Publications
Kalamazoo, Michigan

This edition replaces the first edition, which was numbered
Cistercian Studies Series One-hundred Nine

The work of Cistercian Publications is made possible in part
by support from
Western Michigan University
to The Institute of Cistercian Studies

Library of Congress Cataloguing in Publication Data

Bell, David N., 1943–
    A cloud of witnesses : an introduction to the development of
Christian doctrine to AD 500 / by David N. Bell.—2nd rev. ed.
        p.   cm.—(Cistercian studies series ; no. 218)
    Includes index.
    ISBN 978-0-87907-218-6
    1. Theology, Doctrinal—History—Early church, ca.30–600.
I. Title.   II. Series.

BT25.B38   2007
230.09'015—dc22

                                                                2007017829

TABLE OF CONTENTS

PREFACE TO THE SECOND EDITION

IN PREPARING the second edition of this book, I have taken the opportunity of making a multitude of minor amendments and, in certain areas, adding a considerable amount of additional information. This is particularly the case in the chapters dealing with Gnosticism, the Arian controversy, the Christological controversy, the development of the Roman primacy, and the Last Things. I would also point out that, by its very nature, an introductory text such as this must of necessity present the development of Christian doctrine in a rather more logical and cohesive manner than was the case in reality. Putting it another way, the gradual growth of Christian theology was actually much more messy than it appears here.

Whether Christian doctrine ever did develop is another question. Some would say that the Truth, the whole Truth, was always there, like a statue hidden in the rock from which it will eventually emerge, and that slowly, over the centuries, by a gradual process of carving and chipping away, more and more of it has been revealed. The analogy is Plotinian—a philosophical concept we shall talk about later.

Interestingly enough, the question was discussed in the first half of the fifth century by Vincent of Lérins. If the canon of Scripture is perfect, he asked, 'and is in itself sufficient—indeed, more than sufficient—in everything', and if, in interpreting this Scripture, 'we, in the Church Catholic, take the greatest care to hold that which has been believed everywhere, always, and by all', then what room is there for progress (*profectus*) in the Church of Christ?[1] His answer

---

1. Vincent of Lérins, *Commonitorium,* II.5-6.

is clear: there is certainly room for progress, but only when progress means a true advance in the faith and not a change (*permutatio*) in the faith. Progress, he says, implies a certain growth and development within a thing itself, while change transforms one thing into something different. Thus, 'the ancient doctrines of heavenly philosophy should, with the course of time, be carefully tended, refined, and polished. They should not be changed, mutilated, or lessened. They may certainly gain clarity, light, and distinctness, but they must also retain their completeness, integrity, and characteristic quality.'[2]

It is not difficult to appreciate Vincent's point, but the question of whether (taking but one example) the Christological transition from the Jesus of the New Testament—Jesus the wonder-working rabbi—to the God-man, the *theanthrōpos,* the divine Christ of later Alexandrian theology, is an advance or a change is a matter for the judgement of the individual reader.

Finally, the illustrations in this second edition are entirely new. The first edition had only line drawings and inadequate captions. That is no longer the case. Apart from photographs of monuments and sites, the text is illustrated with photographs of modern Orthodox icons painted by Eileen McGuckin, who now has her studio and permanent gallery at The Icon Studio in New York. She grew up in the north of England and came to New York in 1997, by which time she had received the official blessing of the Romanian Orthodox Church to be an ecclesiastical icon-painter in the Byzantine and Slavonic traditions. She now works full-time as a professional iconographer, and her work has featured in a number of books, both in Europe and America. It is a privilege to be able to reproduce some of her paintings here. An icon, we might add, is not merely a religious picture, but a statement of theology, and those interested in reading more on this matter may be referred to Chapter 14 in the companion volume to this present study, *Many Mansions. An Introduction to the Development and Diversity of Medieval Theology West and East* (Kalamazoo-Spencer, 1996).

D.N.B.

2. *Ibid.,* XXIII.54, 57.

This is the most common icon of Christ and depicts him as the 'All-Sovereign' or 'Ruler of All', *Pantokrator* in Greek. The icon shows Christ as judge, the Alpha and Omega of the Book of Revelation, 'He who is and who was and who is to come, the All-Sovereign' (Rev 1:8). In his left hand he carries a closed book, and his right hand is raised in blessing. To the left and right of his halo we see his name, ı< ēsou>s ch<risto>s or 'Jesus Christ', and in the halo itself are the Greek words <h>o ōn, 'He who is'. This is the name which God revealed to Moses on Mount Horeb (Ex 3:14), and it is also one of the titles of Christ in Revelation 1:8. In other words, the title 'He who is' tells us that God the Father and God the Son are two Persons, but one single substance in the unity of the Trinity.

CHRIST PANTOCRATOR

Icon by Eileen McGuckin
Location: The Icon Studio, New York
Photo: Eileen McGuckin

PREFACE

THIS LITTLE BOOK is not intended to be a substitute for such excellent volumes as J. N. D. Kelly's *Early Christian Doctrines* (1968 [fourth edition]), or the first volume of Jaroslav Pelikan's *The Christian Tradition: A History of the Development of Doctrine* (1971), or even for the old but sound survey by J. F. Bethune-Baker, *An Introduction to the Early History of Christian Doctrine* (1903). It is, instead, intended to be an introduction to such works as these, laying the foundations for their more detailed investigation, and preparing the ground for their more thorough examination. It is a book in which footnotes have been virtually eliminated (those that are to be found are restricted almost entirely to primary sources, and all translations are my own), in which Greek and Latin terms have been severely curtailed, and in which the multitudinous and colourful *dramatis personae* of early Christian doctrinal history have been reduced, if not to a minimum, at least to a workable number. It is intended not for the specialist or the scholar, but simply for anyone interested in learning something about the way in which the doctrines of early Christianity developed.

It is also a book in which the reader will find two different styles of writing—one colloquial and one literary—a large number of analogies drawn from everyday life, and, in some cases, what some may consider to be a somewhat impious attitude to the sacred truths of the Christian religion. Perhaps, then, one should say a word or two about these matters. First, to write in a uniform style is simple, but soporific; and since many of the early fathers had little hesitation in using colloquialisms, neither have I. Secondly, some of the analogies may be thought by some to be a little earthy. But as all of us are or should be aware, the most rarefied truths may often be expressed in very earthy language. The Bible itself is sufficient witness to this principle. Thirdly, impiety, like beauty, may well be in the eye of the beholder. The views and opinions of the early fathers range, like the ideas of most of humanity, from the sublime to the ridiculous, and if some of the ideas are indeed just plain silly, it would be dishonest and misleading not to say so. The Sufi tradition rightly maintains that one cannot teach a person who has no sense of humour (few nowadays would subscribe to the view of Saint John Chrysostom that Christ never laughed), and those who have none should not read this book.

Simplification has, of course, been essential. As I said earlier, this is merely an introduction to patristic studies, not a comprehensive examination of what is a vast and ever-growing field of study. It has not been possible, therefore, to deal with all the details and ramifications of, let us say, the Christological controversy and its aftermath, for not only are the political and ecclesiastical complexities themselves too difficult for a book of this nature, but a full understanding of the matter demands a working knowledge of at least Greek and Latin (and preferably Syriac and Coptic), and not everyone has time to acquire this. Simplification, however, is also dangerous, and if I have on occasion lapsed into over-simplification (a euphemism for inaccuracy) I am sure that my reviewers will point it out.

If this volume is found to be too brief, longer studies (such as those already mentioned) are easily available; and as Oliver Goldsmith said:

Good people all, of every sort,
Give ear unto my song;
And if you find it wond'rous short,
It cannot hold you long.

This marble head, over eight feet in height, is one of the surviving fragments of a huge seated statue of the emperor Constantine I (d. 337) which was originally placed in the Basilica Nova of Maxentius and Constantine in the Roman Forum. The head, hands, and feet—the exposed parts—were made of marble, while the rest of the body (which would have been magnificently robed) was of less valuable materials. The complete statue was about thirty feet high, and its grandeur and size clearly testify to Constantine's sense of his own importance.

COLOSSAL HEAD OF CONSTANTINE THE GREAT

Location: Musei Capitolini, Rome
Photo: Terryl N. Kinder

1

AN HISTORICAL OUTLINE

TO UNDERSTAND and appreciate the course of Christianity

and the development of Christian ideas over the first five centuries,

the reader must keep in mind a few major events and major dates.

The history of the first centuries of Christianity may, for the sake

of simplicity, be divided into five main periods, as follows: (1) from

the death of Jesus of Nazareth to 250: the beginnings of persecu-

tion; (2) from 250 to 311: the period of systematic persecution;

(3) from 311 to 325: the rise of Constantine; (4) from 325 to 392:

the triumph of imperial Christianity; and (5) from 392 to the end of

the fifth century: the division of the Roman Empire. Let us glance

very briefly at each of these periods in turn.

1. The Beginnings of Persecution

After the execution of Jesus of Nazareth, Christianity, primarily through the efforts of Paul and his followers, spread from Palestine to the gentile world of the Mediterranean. The ruler of the Mediterranean world at this time was Rome, and to a large extent therefore the early history of Christianity becomes a history of its dealings with the Roman administration.

The Romans, on the whole, were remarkably tolerant in the matter of religion and, with very few exceptions, left their citizens to worship whatever gods or goddesses they preferred in whatever way they desired, *provided*—and it is a very important proviso—that they also worshipped the emperor. 'Worship', however, is a misleading term, especially as the word is used nowadays. The rite itself was simple. It might demand, for example, no more than burning a pinch of incense before a statue of the emperor—and was regarded by the majority of Roman administrators more as a political than a religious gesture. That is, it was seen as a religio-political ritual by which one indicated one's affiliation to the Roman Empire and one's recognition of the Roman emperor as the legitimate ruler. Putting it another way, it indicated that one was prepared to render unto Caesar the things that were Caesar's.

Only the Jews were exempt from this requirement, and so long as Christianity was viewed as a Jewish sect, it could claim the same exemption. But as soon as Christianity saw itself, and was seen, as a separate and distinct religion, the Romans naturally required of the Christians all that they required of the other religious groups in the empire, including the 'worship' or formal recognition of its legally constituted ruler. It was, for the most part, a sort of early pledge of allegiance.

This the Christians refused to do, not because they would not acknowledge the emperor (they were, in fact, some of the most law-abiding citizens of the empire and had been instructed by Saint Paul to obey all authorities ordained by God[1]), but because they considered the rite to be a denial of the basic Christian principle

---

1. Rom 13:1-6.

that the only object of worship could and should be the one God. In other words, the Christians, for primarily *religious* reasons, refused to participate in a rite which, for primarily *political* reasons, was required of all by Rome.

The consequences of this were as inevitable as they were unfortunate: the Christians were suspected of treason against the state, of refusing to acknowledge the emperor, and of denying the legitimacy of Roman authority. And, in addition to this, the Christian communities in Rome and elsewhere had become generally disliked and suspected within twenty years of the death of Jesus of Nazareth. The reasons for this will be considered in detail a little later, but suffice it to say for the moment that the Christians were regarded as exclusive and secretive sectarian groups who were convinced that they were better than everyone else, and who participated in religious rituals which were, to say the least, highly suspect. It is all very well for a modern Christian to speak of 'eating the flesh' and 'drinking the blood' of Christ: everyone knows that the language is here allegorical or symbolic. But the average Roman of the first century heard the words literally and drew the obvious though mistaken conclusion that Christians were cannibals.

The result was persecution, but until about the middle of the third century, persecution was local and sporadic. It would flare up in one city or region for a month or a year or more and then simmer down, only to flare up again in another city elsewhere. There were, however, two persecutions of considerable duration and violence: those of Nero (from 54 to 68) and of Trajan (from 98 to 117). Yet continual, widespread, and systematic persecution did not occur until the second half of the third century: the second period in this very brief history.

2. Systematic Persecution

During the later third and early fourth centuries, the Roman Empire underwent a series of crises, some political, some military, some economic—and many which were all three. The internal unity of the empire was threatened and there was general unrest and dissension. It was not difficult, in these troubled times, to see the Christians—the disliked, distrusted, secretive, exclusive Christians who refused to worship the emperor—as being at or near the source of these very serious disorders. The Roman administration, in fact, tended to regard Christians in much the same light as Jews were regarded in Nazi Germany, and the fact that the Christians themselves were innocent of almost all the accusations levied against them was quite irrelevant. Then as now, it was what people believed which was important, and there is no doubt that people often believed the worst of the Christians and frequently treated them as scapegoats.

The first general legislation against the Christians was enacted in 249, when the emperor Decius demanded that all his subjects should make the appropriate sacrifice to the emperor and obtain an official certificate that they had done so. Anyone who refused would suffer. And suffer they did. But this general persecution fizzled out with the defeat and death of Decius in 251, and although a subsequent emperor—Valerian—reintroduced a more limited period of persecution in the late 250s, it was not until the later years of the emperor Diocletian, some forty years in the future, that systematic persecution was resumed.

The consequences of this intensified persecution, however, were not quite what the persecutors intended. Instead of annihilating Christianity and destroying its communities, the external threat served rather to unite and bind the Christians more strongly together. And there can be no doubt that the extraordinary courage of many of the early martyrs gave hope, confidence, and encouragement to those who had not yet suffered. Under these conditions petty rivalries were forgotten and local disputes dwindled into insignificance, and there is a great deal of truth in the famous statement attributed to Tertullian that the blood of the martyrs was the seed of the Church.[2]

The last of the great persecutions was that of Diocletian, whom we mentioned above. He ruled from 284 to 305 and seems to have

---

2. What Tertullian actually said was simply 'the seed is the blood of Christians' (*Apologeticus*, 50).

believed that the formal practice of the old Roman pagan religion was essential if Rome was to retain divine protection. Thus, in 299, he began to purge the court and the army of Christians; in 303 he demanded that churches be destroyed and copies of the Christian scriptures burned; and in a series of later edicts he unleashed a wholesale and brutal persecution of Christians throughout the whole of the empire.

This grim period was brought to a welcome close by an important decree passed by the successor of Diocletian, the emperor Galerius (305–311)—he was Diocletian's coadjutor in the East, but the politics need not here concern us—who, upon his deathbed, gave his sanction to the so-called *Edict of Toleration*. He did so, not out of love for the Christians (whom he hated) or from admiration for their faith (which he despised), but for reasons utilitarian and political. Since, at the time, he was dying from an unpleasant and painful disease, he hoped that Christian prayers might have more success than pagan medicines; and (more importantly) faced with the threat of an alliance between two rival claimants to the imperial throne, he found it politically expedient to conciliate the Christians—and not the least of the reasons for this conciliatory move was that one of these two rival claimants was the charismatic Constantine.

3. THE RISE OF CONSTANTINE

Constantine (between 272 and 288–377) had seen service both at the court of Diocletian and with the Roman army in England, and in the year 306 was proclaimed *imperator* or 'emperor' at York. His claim to the purple was not, however, uncontested. Only in 312, just after the death of Galerius, did he defeat his rival, Maxentius, at the famous battle of the Milvian Bridge, just outside Rome, and achieve his ambition to become senior ruler of the Roman Empire. In that battle, Constantine had fought under the sign of the cross, but the sign of the cross was later modified to form the *labarum,* a word of uncertain etymology. The *labarum* appears to have been a regular Roman cavalry standard with the old pagan symbols removed and the first two letters of the name of Christ (in Greek ΧΡΙΣΤΟΣ =

CHRISTOS) substituted for them: that is, X (the Greek letter chi for CH)
and P (the Greek letter rho for R). The two letters were combined
to form the symbol ☧ or *chi-rho*.

Constantine saw clearly the political advantage of having the
Christians with him rather than against him, and was determined
to link the secular state with the Christian church in the strongest
possible way. In 313, therefore, he reinforced the Edict of Toleration
passed by Galerius by issuing the so-called Edict of Milan, though
the precise nature and legal status of these 'edicts' need not concern
us. The new edict declared that all religions, including Christianity,
were to be tolerated equally, and recognized the full legal existence
of the Christian churches.

The question as to whether Constantine himself was truly Christian is difficult to answer. He obviously (and wisely) preferred to have
a foot in the pagan camp as well as the Christian, and although he
was baptized into the Christian faith just before his death, there is
no doubt that his Christianity sat but lightly on his shoulders. Nor
did his conduct in later life accord particularly well with the ethical
principles of the New Testament. Among other acts of questionable
morality, he arranged for the judicial murder of his wife, Fausta (according to a somewhat dubious tradition, she was suffocated in an
over-heated Roman bath), and one of his sons.

On the other hand, he certainly admired Christianity and was
certainly influenced by it. Under Constantine there was a humani-
zation of the criminal law, an amelioration in the position of slaves,
improvements in the situation of the poor, and a considerable number of benefits accorded to Christian churches and clergy. It was
Constantine, too, who, in 321, commanded that Sunday (with typical
Constantinean ambivalence, the 'Sun-day' and the 'Son-day') should
be a public holiday, and it was also Constantine who determined
that his newly-won empire should have a new imperial seat: the
city of Constantinople (the name means 'Constantine's City'). It was
inaugurated as the imperial capital in 330 and remained the capital
of the eastern empire until 1453 when it was captured by the Turks
and renamed Istanbul.

With Constantine's protection and encouragement, therefore,
Christianity flourished, but the consequences were not wholly for-

tunate. Now that the external threat had been removed, the Christians could devote themselves to what was clearly becoming their predominant interest: arguing among themselves on a multitude of theological points—some minor, some major. Undoubtedly the most important quarrel to arise concerned the doctrine of the Trinity. The causes of this great controversy, the points at issue, and its ultimate resolution we shall consider in due course, but for our immediate purposes we need only note that the disagreements (disagreements, primarily, about the place occupied by God the Son in relation to God the Father) were sufficiently deep and sufficiently intense to split the Church into two warring camps and threaten Constantine's newly-gained empire with major civil discord.

Something, obviously, had to be done, and done with all possible speed. So Constantine called a council to decide the issue, a council which would be attended (at least in theory) by representatives from the whole Christian world and which would be held under his watchful eye at Nicaea (now the town of Iznik in modern Turkey, not far from Istanbul) in the early summer of the year 325. This was the First General or Ecumenical Council, and we shall discuss its full significance later. The term 'ecumenical' derives from a Greek word meaning 'the civilized world', and for the Greeks, the civilized world was the world around the shores of the Mediterranean.

4. THE TRIUMPH OF IMPERIAL CHRISTIANITY

The decades following the Council of Nicaea in 325 were marked by continuing theological discord, and it took some fifty years before the tensions aroused by this first great dispute finally subsided. But these years were marked by the rapid consolidation of Christianity and a corresponding diminution in the importance and influence of paganism. The efforts of the emperor Julian—called by the Christians Julian the Apostate—who in his short reign (361–363) attempted to reintroduce the pagan cults and degrade, if not extirpate, Christianity, utterly failed to stem the irresistible tide, and the story that Julian died with the words *'Vicisti Galilæe'* ('Thou hast conquered, Galilean') on his lips, while historically inaccurate, is a fair reflection of the course of events. The matter came to a head in the year 392, when the emperor Theodosius I made the teaching of heresy a legal offence, outlawed paganism, prohibited sacrifice, and, to all intents and purposes, established Christianity as the only legal religion of the Roman Empire.

The consequences of this momentous decision were not altogether favourable. Many who had never had either the taste or the inclination for orthodox Christianity now 'discovered' that in their hearts they had been Christian all the time. The Christian church and the Christian state, which had been converging since the time of Constantine, now became virtually indistinguishable. Bishops became high dignitaries of state with magisterial functions. The Church acquired immense riches and huge tracts of lands. Churches themselves grew larger and larger and more and more splendid. And hand-in-hand with this ever-increasing magnificence, the liturgy became more protracted, more complex, more elaborate, and more beautiful. Inevitably, however, this increase in wealth and power produced a corresponding increase in corruption, and despite a number of truly saintly figures, the Church of the fourth century was a hotbed of intrigue, political machination, dispute, and disagreement. Some would say, in fact, that the two worst things that happened to Christianity during its first four hundred years were the end of active persecution and the elevation of the religion to the position of the official state cult.

5. The Division of the Roman Empire

The Christian empire of Theodosius I was no longer a harmonious and united whole. Since the time of Constantine—indeed, for some years before his reign—the huge geographical mass of the Roman world had been splitting in two. Cultural, linguistic, and political differences instituted a process which led eventually to an Eastern Roman Empire, with Greek as its official language and Constantinople its capital, and a Western Roman Empire, with Latin as its official language and its capital first at Rome and later at Milan and Ravenna. The Eastern Empire encompassed Greece, Asia Minor (i.e.

modern Turkey), Syria, Palestine, Egypt, and the whole eastern half
of the Mediterranean. The Western Empire included Italy, North
Africa, Spain, Gaul, Germany, and Britain.

This division was accentuated in the fifth century by a series of
invasions which devastated much of western Europe, including Italy,
during this period. Rome itself was sacked twice. Most of the invaders
belonged to Germanic tribes—Goths, Ostrogoths, Visigoths, Vandals,
and the like. Some of these so-called barbarians were at least nominally
Christian. Some, including the ferocious Huns under their leader
Attila—who were Asians, coming from areas north of the Caspian
Sea—were not. But whether Christian, semi-Christian, or pagan, these
nomadic invaders brought on the economic and political collapse of
the western half of the empire, and the elevation to a position of major
importance of the bishops of Rome.

Up to the time of Constantine, the power of the popes had been
very limited; but with the ever-increasing importance of Christianity
and, most especially, the barbarian invasions of the fifth century, papal
power increased enormously. The popes were seen as firm rocks in
a political and social quicksand and presented to the western eye
one of the few stable and, so it would appear, enduring institutions
in conditions which all too frequently approached anarchy. And
the popes themselves, whether they liked it or not (some did; some
did not), were forced to extend their jurisdiction from the realm of
the ecclesiastical to that of the secular. One thing is certain: from
the middle of the fifth century onwards, the papacy could not be
ignored, and from the time of Leo I, called Leo the Great (who
died in 461), the Roman see, fully consolidated, enjoyed enormous
prestige, influence, and importance.

The situation in the Greek-speaking east was strikingly different.
With the exception of an early incursion by the Goths, the barbarian
invasions generally petered out at the borders of Greece. The Eastern
Roman Empire, with its imperial seat in Constantinople, was not subjected to prolonged and catastrophic change until the rise of Muslim
power in the seventh and eighth centuries. In the relative security of
the Christian east, the theological disputes which were so congenial
to the Greek mind flourished and blossomed with remarkable vigour.
Paramount among the disputes was no longer the question of the

Trinity—that had been settled by about 380—but the question of the person of Christ: more precisely, the question of how the divine and human parts of this unique being were united or conjoined in Jesus of Nazareth. It was this dispute—more complex and yet more bitter than that over the Trinity—which led the emperor of the time, like Constantine before him, to call a council (more accurately a series of councils) to attempt to settle the issue. The end result of these endeavours was the great Council of Chalcedon, the Fourth Ecumenical Council, which met in Chalcedon (almost opposite Constantinople on the other shore of the Bosphorus) on 8 October 451 and which, like the Council of Nicaea, we shall examine in detail in due course.

What happened in east and west after the fifth century need not for the moment concern us. If we bear in mind the dates of the 'edicts of toleration', of the Council of Nicaea, of the establishment of Christianity as the official religion of the Roman Empire, and of the Council of Chalcedon, we shall find this an adequate basis for the discussions to follow. Let us now, therefore, turn from history to philosophy and examine the intellectual and philosophical background against which Christian doctrine developed.

The Neo-Platonist Plotinus (*c*. 205–270) was the greatest of the later Platonic philosophers. This marble sarcophagus, dating from the late third or early fourth century, may once have contained his body, but that cannot be regarded as certain. The sculpted scene certainly shows a philosopher teaching his pupils, both female and male, but we cannot be sure of the philosopher's identity.

SARCOPHAGUS, SAID TO BE THAT OF PLOTINUS

Location: Museo Gregoriano Profano, Vatican Museums, Vatican State
Photo: Scala/Art Resource, New York

II

THE INTELLECTUAL BACKGROUND

THE IMMEDIATE DISCIPLES of Jesus of Nazareth were, of course, converts: converts from Judaism. Similarly, the earliest Christians to appear in the gentile world were also converts: converts in this case from one or other of the rich diversity of religions with which the Graeco-Roman world was so adequately stocked. But with any convert, it is as important—perhaps more important—to understand what they converted *from* as what they converted *to*; for any person moving from one tradition to another will understand and interpret the concepts of the latter by the familiar intellectual suppositions of the former. In psychological terms, we would call it transfer of training. It is essential, therefore, to appreciate the way in which these early converts thought, for it was they who were to become the presbyters and bishops of the Christian churches, and it was they who were responsible for the creation and development of Christian doctrine.

We need not here concern ourselves with every mode of thought to be found within the wide reaches of the Roman Empire, but only with the three which most deeply influenced the development of Christian theology: the philosophies of Stoicism and Platonism, and that curious and eclectic collection of loosely connected sects generally known as Gnosticism. Let us begin with Stoicism.

1. STOICISM

Stoicism was a school of thought founded at Athens in the fourth century BCE by Zeno of Citium (335–263 BCE). Its viewpoint was entirely materialistic. Unlike Platonism—and, later, Christianity—it denied any separate world of 'spirit' and maintained that there existed only matter. Even its concept of God was not of a Supreme Being, spiritual and immaterial, but only of a more refined and subtle form of matter, a sort of formless gaseous fire which permeated all things as water permeates a sponge or light permeates air. Yet this 'gaseous fire' was also rational and intelligent: it was not only immanent in all things, bound them together, and made them what they were, but it also ordered them in their courses and directed them to their proper ends. Because of this all-pervading 'spirit' or 'god', the law of nature and the law of duty are incumbent upon all things. Because of it puppies turn into dogs, and not into cats or jelly-fish, the seasons follow one another in their appointed round, and seeds produce plants which produce fruit which, in turn, produce further seeds. And as for human beings, the ideal way for them is also to 'live according to rational nature', and by this the Stoics understood that the entirety of one's life should be governed by reason, not emotion, and that 'rational action' was the only proper action for a rational being. If we consider how often we act by emotion, instinct, desire, lust, and greed (and one need only watch a single episode of the daily soaps to see all this), then we may appreciate a little more clearly how difficult to achieve was the Stoic goal.

Stoic influence on Christianity was confined to two main areas. First, the idea that all human beings are rational and have within them the 'spark of reason' or the 'divine spark'. In later centuries this would be of fundamental importance in developing the biblical idea that every man and woman is created *ad imaginem Dei,* 'in the image of God': i.e. as a rational creature with God-given free will. Secondly, Stoicism had a considerable impact on the development of Christian ethics. Goodness, for the Stoics, was to be found not in external objects, but in the interior state of the soul. A good person is a person who has conquered the passions and desires which disturb the course of everyday life, and a good person manifests the four cardinal virtues of Stoic philosophy: wisdom, courage, justice, and moderation. Furthermore, since all people are manifestations of the one all-pervading spirit, it follows that there is a natural equality of all human beings, and that all human beings should, ideally, love and help one another. It is a noble concept. But despite the fact that Stoic traces can be clearly discerned in the ideas of a number of theologians of the first three centuries, it was Platonism—especially from the time of Clement of Alexandria, whom we shall meet in Chapter Four—which had a far more profound effect on the making of Christian doctrine, and it is to a consideration of that school of thought to which we may now turn.

2. Platonism

Like Stoicism, this school was also founded at Athens in the fourth century BCE, and in the course of its development from the time of Plato (427–347 BCE) to the time of the Christians it underwent a considerable number of changes. If this were a history of philosophy we would have to distinguish Middle Platonism from Neo-Platonism, but since it is not, and since our interests are not in Platonism itself but in its impact on Christianity, we can try to combine the two together and point out the main features of what we may term simply 'Later Platonism'.

The Platonists, unlike the Stoics, had no doubt as to the real existence of a spiritual realm, and their main concern was to explain, or to try to explain, how this spiritual realm, which is pure, unsullied, and utterly perfect, could possibly be related to this obviously imperfect, impure, unpleasant, polluted, and war-torn world. To appreciate their solution it may help if we imagine a set of traffic signals with the road underneath. Corresponding to the red light at the top was the Source of All Things, which the Platonists generally referred to as The One. This 'One' was there from the beginning: it has no body, no shape, no form, no passions, no needs, no desires. It is simply a 'One-ness', existing eternally, and containing within itself the potentiality for all things. If we may use a human analogy, it corresponds to a creative artist—let us say a potter—in deep sleep. He or she has the *potential* to create all sorts of things—plates, cups, vases, and so on—but at the moment is not doing anything about it. Before anything is actually created, therefore, we must move on to another stage.

This second stage is the amber light of the traffic signal and it corresponds to our artist waking up and thinking 'I shall make a Cup'. In other words, we have now moved from the realm of *potentiality* to the realm of *thought,* but only to the realm of *abstract* thought. That is to say, the artist has simply conceived the idea of 'Cup' and has not thought of any particular cup of a specific shape and a specific size. This second stage of the process was called by the Platonists 'The Divine Mind', and whereas the first stage could be called 'The Infinite Potentiality of God', this second stage could be termed 'God thinking'. It is at this second stage that the One conceives the plan of creation: it thinks 'Cup', 'Cat', 'Dog', 'Truth', 'Justice', 'Tree', and so on. But as we noted earlier, these ideas (and the Divine Mind is often referred to as 'The World of the Ideas') are still abstract, and although the One has now thought 'Dog', there is still a long way to go before we find a specific German Shepherd or Black Labrador running around in search of a fire hydrant.

We must therefore move on to a third stage: the green light on the traffic signal. This stage, to which the Platonists gave the curious title of 'The World-Soul'—for reasons which need not here concern us—, corresponds to the artist who has already thought 'Cup' now determining exactly what sort of cup will be made. We are here concerned with the precise colour, shape, size, and material of the object and have moved from the realm of the *abstract* to the realm of the *concrete* or the *particular*. At this stage of the process, the One is thinking not just of 'Dog', but of all the different varieties of dogs; not just of 'Truth', but of all its multitudinous manifestations. And when these particular and specific thoughts are merged with matter, then we have the world as we see it (this is the road beneath the green light), full of all sorts of things, all sorts of people, all sorts of animals, and all sorts of ideas. The Platonic scheme, therefore, looks something like this:

Potentiality for Dogs (and All Else)	The One	The realm of infinite potentiality
The abstract idea of 'Dog'	The Divine Mind	The realm of the Divine Ideas
The specific idea of Black Labradors	The World-Soul	The realm of specific ideas
A specific female Black Labrador called Tia	The World	The realm of specific things

Only two final points need be made with regard to this scheme: the first is that just as in the set of traffic signals the green is below the amber and the amber below the red, so, too, in Platonism, the second principle, the Divine Mind, is lower than and subordinate to the One, and the World-Soul is lower than and subordinate to the Divine Mind. Secondly, every human being is comprised of soul and body, and since the soul is a *spiritual*, not a material, entity, its true home is not here in this material world, but in the spiritual world of the Divine Mind. The soul, therefore, which is in essence something pure and perfect, has 'fallen' in some way from its true home and has become enmeshed or imprisoned or entombed in flesh and matter. One of the most famous sayings of the Platonists was 'The body is a tomb' (*ho sōma sēma*: the phrase sounds better in Greek), indicating

the way in which they viewed the plight of humanity. They saw the
soul (if we may change the metaphor) as a bird in a cage, waiting
only for the door to be opened before it could fly free, soaring up
and up, alone to the Alone, back to the perfection and purity from
which it came. The fundamental impact of this way of thinking on
the development of the Christian doctrine of the Trinity will become
clear in the next few chapters.

3. GNOSTICISM

The third of the three schools of thought we shall consider is Gnosticism, and it would be well to appreciate from the beginning that the
term does not refer to one specific school alone, but to a whole collection of sectarian groups, frequently mutually antagonistic, which
differed dramatically from each other in the details of their beliefs.
Some of their beliefs are impressive, some are curious, and some are
quite extraordinary; but despite their manifold differences all were
agreed upon three basic points.

Firstly, they were all Platonic in the sense that they all saw this
imperfect world as being separated from the Supreme Being or the
Source of All Things by a series of intermediaries, commonly referred
to as *aeons*. About the number and nature of these intermediaries,
however, there were radical differences of opinion. Some (like the
Platonists) maintained there were but few; others (like the Alexandrian Gnostic, Basilides) held that they totalled three hundred and
sixty-five. But however many there were, they all had their own
names and characteristics, and for reasons which will become clear
in a moment, these names were of the utmost importance.

Secondly, all the Gnostic groups were Platonic in the sense that
they all saw the human soul as being a perfect—or at least a moder-
ately perfect—entity entrapped and entombed in flesh. And all were
agreed that it had to be released from its prison and directed back
to its true home. As to how this was to be done, the various groups
were, again, at odds. Most people, of course, were quite unaware that
they were 'souls imprisoned'—the Gnostics called these unfortunates
'sleep-walkers' and included by the term almost everyone who was

not a Gnostic—but even if these sleepers could be roused from their somnambulant condition, further difficulties awaited them. Why? Because the various intermediaries or *aeons* would, if possible, try to prevent the soul from returning to its source, and unless each *aeon* could be controlled and overcome, the soul would never achieve its goal. The situation can be likened to a Jacob's ladder, set between earth and heaven, with each of its dozens of rungs being guarded by an antagonistic and/or malignant being. How, then, could these *aeons* be controlled? The answer was simple: by knowing their names. Knowledge of their names gave one total power over them, and the various sects therefore entrusted to their members, under terms of the utmost secrecy, the true spellings and sounds of these appellations. That none of the various groups agreed with each other as to the nature of these names or their number need not here concern us and should cause us no surprise. But how were these names revealed in the beginning? Who taught the Gnostic teachers what they needed to know? The answer to this question leads us to the third and final point we need to consider.

Thirdly, all the Gnostic groups were agreed that liberation, or redemption, was a possibility: that it was possible for us to 'wake up', free our souls from our bodies, and negotiate successfully the perilous path which leads to our spiritual home. They also agreed that at certain times there had appeared redeemers who had revealed to us all the information that was necessary. The identity of these redeemers differed, as we might expect, according to the sect concerned. Some Gnostics, for example, suggested that the most important redeemer/revealer had been Simon Magus (the magician of Acts 8); others preferred Hercules. But a considerable number, though by no means all, viewed the redeemer as Jesus Christ. Christ had appeared on earth and revealed to the ignorant faithful, to the 'ordinary' Christians, the truths in the four canonical gospels, but these truths were no more than the pablum of the nursery. To the Gnostics he had revealed far more: the true meat of the doctrine, suitable for adults endowed with reason and courage. And the Gnostics could produce a large number of non-canonical Gospels and other treatises to prove it. The best known of these apocryphal gospels is the Gospel of Thomas, a work originally written in Greek in the middle of the

second century, which contains more than a hundred sayings and
brief discourses attributed to Jesus. Some of these can be paralleled
in the four gospels of the New Testament; some cannot, and it is
quite possible—indeed, probable—that some of the sayings may well
reproduce a genuine oral tradition. One of the most celebrated is
'Split a piece of wood and I am there; lift a stone and you will find
me'.[1] But ideas like this are undoubtedly dangerous. If God is to
be found under stones and in birch junks, what need is there for a
sacramental Church and an intermediary priesthood?

Many of the Gnostic writings, however, are much more obscure,
as is sometimes indicated by their titles. A large cache of documents,
all in Coptic, was discovered between 1945–1946 at Nag Hammadi
in Upper Egypt (about sixty miles south of Luxor), and although
this treasure-trove included the *Gospel of Thomas* and the *Gospel of
Truth,* both of which are fairly close to orthodoxy, it also included
the *Hypostasis of the Archons, Eugnostos the Blessed,* the *Paraphrase of
Seth, The Three Steles of Seth, The Thought of Norea, Hypsiphrone,* and
the *Trimorphic Protennoia.*[2] Some of these writings contain ideas of
formidable complexity. Many contain ideas which could never have
been countenanced by the early Church. *The Gospel of the Egyptians,*
for example, has the indescribable Source of All Things, 'the Father
of Silence', producing a Trinity of Father, Mother, and Son. This
was hardly biblical and, in any case, it seems that one of the many
things that the early Christian Fathers objected to about Gnosticism
was its positive evaluation of women and what we might call the
Feminine Principle.

Again, in the *Gospel of Philip,* we learn of a far more intimate
relationship between Jesus and Mary Magdalene than ever appears
in Matthew, Mark, Luke, or John. Mary is spoken of as the 'companion' or 'partner' of Jesus (the Coptic text borrows the Greek word
koinōnos), and we are told that Christ loved her more than any of the

---

1. *Gospel of Thomas,* Saying 77.
2. Translations of all the documents are to be found in J. M. Robinson, ed.,
The Nag Hammadi Library in English (New York, 1977, 1990).

other disciples and would kiss her more often.[3] And of even greater impact in the same gospel is what appears, at first glance, to be a clear denial of the Christian doctrine of the resurrection: 'Those who say that first the Lord died and then arose are mistaken, for first he arose, and then he died.'[4] This certainly seems to support the theory, advanced by some modern scholars, that Jesus did not die on the cross. He was, on the contrary, taken down alive, went on to live many more years, and eventually died the ordinary death of an ordinary human being. This, however, is not what the *Gospel of Philip* means, and it is a good example of the danger of taking such quotations out of context. The meaning, as is clear from other sections of the same gospel, is that the Lord 'arose' at the time of his baptism in the Jordan, when the Holy Spirit descended upon him and transformed him from a human being into the Divine Redeemer. Before that moment he was Jesus; after that moment he was the Lord. Then, when he was crucified a few years later, his human body died and the divine Spirit or Power which possessed him returned to its source. In other words, the *Gospel of Philip* is not denying that Jesus died on the cross, though some other Gnostic groups were certainly prepared to do so. According to them, it was not Jesus who died, but a substitute—usually seen as Simon of Cyrene—and the real Jesus was observing the events from afar, laughing. Such was the view of Basilides, the Gnostic teacher whom we mentioned earlier. And as to the events which led up to the crucifixion, the Gnostic *Gospel of Judas* puts the arch-villain of mainstream Christianity in a totally new—and wholly positive—light.

As far as many of the Gnostics were concerned, this was really what had happened, this was what Christ was really like, and this was what he had taught. *This* was the true Christianity. It was not a system which asked only simple faith, but a system which demanded intellectual understanding and secret knowledge; a system not for

3. *Gospel of Philip*, 59, 63–64. The gospel probably dates from the second half of the third century.

4. *Ibid.*, 56. The gospel also denies (*ibid.*, 55) that Mary conceived by the Holy Spirit.

the many, but for the few; a system not for sleep-walkers, but for spiritual athletes; a system not for believers, but for those who had the courage to be *knowers*. And 'knower' is what 'Gnostic' means: they knew the history of creation, they knew why we are as we are, they knew the nature of the prison, they knew the truth about Jesus and his teachings, they knew the way out, and they knew the pass-words which would open all doors. They knew, in short, the way home and how to get there. And there is no doubt that their knowledge was much esteemed and that Gnosticism was very popular. There is no doubt, too, that it was both feared and disliked by the Fathers of the Church.

One of the reasons for this dislike certainly entailed numbers. Early Christianity was eager to proselytise, but the pseudo-Christian Gnostic sects could frequently offer a religious system which was decidedly more attractive and far more intellectually stimulating than early Christianity. They could offer a guaranteed way to salvation; they were often far more similar to the pagan systems which the converts were thinking of leaving; and they could combine all this with the idea of a 'secret' knowledge known only to the elect, and therefore provide their adherents with that sense of superiority, of being so much better than one's fellows, which human beings of all ages have found so dangerously attractive. If, then, pagans who were dissatisfied with the prevailing systems were looking elsewhere, there was a very good chance that when faced with a choice between 'gnostic' Christianity and 'orthodox' Christianity, they would choose the former, and in this way (so far as the 'orthodox' were concerned) the converts would deprive themselves of the hope of salvation and the 'true' Church of the advantage of numbers.

For this, and for other reasons, the Christian pastors of the first two centuries were forced to keep a continual eye—two eyes, in fact—on the progress of Gnosticism, and until it began to fade away in the later third century, it was regarded by the Church Fathers as one of the greatest, if not the greatest, danger to the truth of the faith.

Of these three schools of thought—Stoicism, Platonism, and Gnosticism—it was unquestionably the second which had the most profound impact on Christian doctrine. Stoicism, as we have re-marked, certainly affected Christian ethics and certain aspects of what we might call Christian psychology. Gnosticism was, in general, a threat and a rival rather than an influence. But Platonism formed and moulded the most fundamental and distinctive principle of Christian belief: the doctrine of the Trinity. To see how and why this occurred we must now turn our attention away from the philosophers and the Gnostics to the early Christian Fathers themselves.

This scratched depiction of a man worshipping a crucified donkey probably dates from the beginning of the third century and was discovered on the wall of a former guard-room on the Palatine Hill in Rome in 1857. The Greek text below the image reads ALEXAMENOS SEBETE THEON, 'Alexamenos worships god', and both Alexamenos and the person who made the graffito may well have been Roman soldiers. It accurately reflects the pagan opinion that Christianity was just plain stupid (see Chapter Three).

AN EARLY ANTI-CHRISTIAN GRAFFITO

Location: Palatine Antiquarium Museum, Rome
Image: Scala / Art Resources, New York

III

THE APOSTOLIC FATHERS
AND THE DEFENDERS OF THE FAITH

THE FIRST CHRISTIAN WRITERS to engage our attention are two groups of people who ranged in time from the later years of the first century to the end of the second. One group, the Apostolic Fathers, were Christians writing to Christians; the other group, the Apologists, were Christians writing to non-Christians. Because of this difference, what they say and the way in which they say it are quite distinct. Let us glance at the Apostolic Fathers first.

This name has been given since the latter part of the seventeenth century to a group of writers which includes Clement of Rome, Ignatius of Antioch, Polycarp of Smyrna, Hermas, Papias, and three or four others who have left us written records, but whose precise names and identities are obscure. They were called 'apostolic' either because they were in immediate contact with the apostles themselves or because they received instruction from the apostles' disciples. The letters they wrote are in many ways very similar to the letters we find in the New Testament (indeed, some of their writings were considered to be part of the New Testament canon by certain churches at certain times), and, like many letter-writers, they addressed specific problems which had developed in specific places on specific occasions.

Clement of Rome (*fl. c.* 96), the second or third successor of St Peter (the early lists differ), for example, wrote to the church at Corinth to try to resolve an acrimonious dispute which had led to the deposition of a number of presbyters. Bring them back, he says, and repent! God requires due and proper order in all things, and legitimate authority must be obeyed. And apart from providing us with some very valuable insights into the structure and operation of the Christian ministry of his time, Clement's letter is the earliest example we have of the intervention of the church of Rome in the affairs of the church of another city. We shall say more on this matter in Chapter Fourteen.

Ignatius (*c.* 35–*c.* 107), the highly-strung bishop of Antioch, became caught up in the persecution of Trajan and to his great delight (for he was unnaturally eager for martyrdom) was condemned to die in Rome. He was led from his home city to the capital under a guard of ten soldiers, and on the way he wrote a number of letters to various churches, including one to Rome in which he beseeches the Roman Christians not to intervene with the pagan administration and deprive him of his martyrdom. In these writings we see a deep concern with the reality of the Incarnation (Christ was truly God and truly man, says Ignatius; he was truly born, truly suffered, truly died, and truly redeemed us) and also with the unity of the Church, which, as we have seen, was being threatened by persecution. How can this unity be best assured? Look to the bishop! says Ignatius. There is one church, one eucharist, one sanctuary, one faith, one bishop. Look to him; give heed to him; follow him; obey him. Without him, there shall be no Baptism; without him, no Eucharist. 'But whatever he approves, that is also well-pleasing to God.'[1] These ideas of Ignatius were important in the later development of the so-called 'monarchical episcopate'—the principle that a local church should be governed by a single bishop in whom all authority is vested—and his views on the person of Christ we shall refer to again in Chapter Eight.

But for all their importance in their own time and place, these Apostolic Fathers were not systematic theologians, and their ideas were not always in conformity with what the Church would later define as 'orthodox'. Indeed, whether we may refer to them as 'theologians' at all is a point which may be debated. And although they were not without significance in such areas as we have outlined above, their contribution to what are undoubtedly the two fundamental doctrines of the Christian tradition—the doctrine of the Trinity and the doctrine of the Person of Christ—was very limited. On these matters they had little to say, and what they did have to say is sometimes decidedly suspect. Hermas, for example, the obscure second-century author of a visionary work called *The Shepherd,* appears to have thought that before Christ became incarnate, he and the Holy Spirit were one and the same, and that the Trinity came into existence only after the humanity of Christ had been taken up into heaven at the Ascension. Before that there was only God the Father and what Hermas calls 'the pre-existent Holy Spirit which created the whole creation'.[2]

To witness the first real developments in Trinitarian thought we must move on to the Apologists, for it was they, speaking not to a Christian but to a pagan world, who found it necessary to explain in some detail concepts which the Apostolic Fathers, Christians writing to Christians, could simply assume.

First of all, the term 'apology' is not being used here in the sense in which we use it today. It meant (and means) in Greek a 'defence', and the Apologists were not saying they were sorry to be Christian. What they were doing was trying to defend the faith against popular

---

1. Ignatius of Antioch, *Letter to the Smyrnaeans,* 8.2.
2. Hermas, *The Shepherd,* Parable 5.6.5 (59).

pagan misunderstandings, Jewish objections, and the very real threat from Gnosticism. The Apologists, of whom there were about a dozen, flourished between about 120 CE and 220 CE, and whereas one or two were Westerners and wrote in Latin (the most important of these being Tertullian, whose ideas we shall consider later), the majority were Greeks. Of these, two are of particular note: Justin Martyr and Irenaeus of Lyons; and we shall confine our examination of the Apologists to these two major figures.

Justin (c. 100–c. 165) was born of pagan parents at the very beginning of the second century, and being possessed of an inquiring mind he worked his way through Stoicism, Aristotelianism, Pythagoreanism, and Platonism before finding his way to Christianity when he was about thirty. He then taught in Ephesus and Rome, and it was there, in about 165, that he and six of his disciples were arraigned before the pagan authorities as Christians. When ordered to sacrifice, and thereby demonstrate their allegiance to the emperor, they all refused, and were accordingly scourged and beheaded. A record of their martyrdom survives, and, unlike many such records, this one is based on official court reports and is far more reliable than most.

Justin, like the other Apologists, was concerned with defending Christianity against popular misunderstandings. What misunderstandings? First, the idea that because Christians refused to 'worship' the emperor they were a danger to the state (we saw how this developed in Chapter One). Secondly, that they were guilty of cannibalism (this, too, we noted in Chapter One). Thirdly, that they indulged in father-daughter incest. This arose because the early Christian Eucharist was called an *agapē,* a Greek word which means literally 'love-feast', and because from the earliest times bishops were referred to as 'father'. If you, as a pagan, heard that someone's daughter was going to a love-feast with her father, what would you think? And fourthly, that Christianity, which apparently worshipped an executed Judaean criminal, was simply superstitious nonsense.

The first three of these misunderstandings were not difficult to counter. The Christians could demonstrate with ease that they were actually some of the most law-abiding citizens of the empire; that when they spoke of the body and blood of Christ, this was not to be taken quite literally; and that a 'love-feast', despite the name (and despite the practices of certain Gnostic sects which turned it into an orgy), was actually a gathering of moral and high-minded Christians in mutual charity and not a lascivious get-together of libidinous perverts indulging in full-frontal nudity and exotic sex. Furthermore, when trying to counter this last misunderstanding, Justin spends some time in telling us what really happened, and in so doing, provides us with an extremely important, though not quite complete, account of a second-century eucharist. We shall say more on this matter in Chapter Fifteen.

We might add, however, that the efforts of the Apologists had only limited usefulness—not because what they wrote was unpersuasive (though reading the rambling prose of Justin is no easy task), but because it is unlikely that many people (particularly those in high places) ever bothered to read it. Justin, as we have seen, was beheaded in about 165, and persecution was to continue for another century and a half.

The fourth accusation (Jewish as well as pagan) was more difficult to counter. Paul had stated the problem long before: 'We preach Christ crucified', he wrote in his first letter to the Corinthians, 'a stumbling-block to the Jews and a folly to the Gentiles' (1 Cor 1:23). And a stumbling-block and folly it remained. The Apologists attempted to deal with the problem in two ways. On the one hand they tried to show that the pagan myths were often even more stupid and foolish than the Christian narrative—this was hardly a wise, and certainly not a successful, approach—and on the other (which was far more positive), they attempted to explain their understanding of Christ and to show how—despite appearances—he was really rather more than an obscure Jewish carpenter who had fallen foul of the Roman authorities. This, inevitably, involved explaining his relationship to the Supreme Being, or, in Christian terms, to God the Father.

Now as we observed earlier, Justin was a convert to Christianity, and the last system to captivate him before his final conversion and baptism had been Later Platonism. It was therefore natural for him to use his Platonism to explain and interpret his Christianity, and, like all other converts from this system, he found that the traffic-signal scheme of the Platonists was ready-made for Christian adaptation and reinterpretation. 'The One' becomes God the Father; the 'Divine Mind' becomes God the Son; and the 'World-Soul' becomes the

Holy Spirit. And although there was some doubt about the third of these equations (the early Christians were even vaguer on the Holy Spirit than were the Platonists on the question of the World-Soul), the first two were clear as day. Unfortunately, however, the Platonic scheme was also a subordinationist scheme—that is, the Divine Mind was subordinate and inferior to the One, and the World-Soul was subordinate and inferior to the Divine Mind—and when Justin applied this scheme to the Christian Trinity, the result was inevitable: God the Son was seen as subordinate and inferior to God the Father. Justin himself states that God the Son is 'second in order', and that the Holy Spirit occupies the third place.[3] But in Justin's time, and for a long period afterwards, no one realized the theological dangers which lurked in this concept.

Platonism, then, imposed upon Christian trinitarianism a subordinationist tendency which was to prove extremely tenacious. But what right had Justin to use the scheme at all? Platonism, after all, was a wholly pagan system, so how could a Christian convert like Justin defend his use of it? Why should Christianity be interpreted by means of paganism? Justin himself realized the importance of this question, and his answer to it is one of his few original contributions to early Christian theology.

The reason, he says, is because the Platonists and other philosophers, together with the Jews, had received their inspiration from Christ. Not, in this case, from Christ *after* his incarnation, but from Christ *before* his incarnation, from Christ the second person of the Trinity, God the Son, who (as Saint John had pointed out) was with the Father in the beginning (Jn 1:2). In other words, God the Son, before he was born of Mary, implanted in the minds of certain individuals seeds of the truth, and as these seeds blossomed and came to fruition, those who had been inspired communicated the truths they had received to the people of their place and time. Plato was one such person in whose mind such seeds had been planted, and so, too, were the prophets of the Old Testament. And what this meant was that Justin did not see three separate sources of inspiration when

3. Justin, *Apologia*, I.xiii.

confronted with three books—the Dialogues of Plato, the Old Testament of the Jews, and the New Testament of the Christians—but three streams deriving from one and the same source: God the Son, who, as he himself said, is Truth (Jn 14: 6). Justin even went so far as to call those who had been inspired in this way 'Christians before Christ', thus making it clear that they had taught the truth even before Truth itself had become incarnate in the person of Jesus of Nazareth. Since, therefore, both Platonism and Judaism had been inspired by God the Son, there was no reason at all why these 'prechristian Christian' writings should not be used to elaborate and explain Christian ideas which came into being after the Incarnation. Later theologians were to refer to this thesis by the curious title of the doctrine of the 'spermatic Logos'. *Logos* is a Greek term meaning 'word' or 'reason', and was the standard term used by theologians of the period to refer to God the Son. It is a splendidly eclectic word, being Platonic, Stoic, and, of course, Christian: 'In the beginning was the Word [*Logos*]' (Jn 1: 1). And *sperma* is the Greek word for 'seed': i.e. the 'seeds of truth' which these early pre-christian Christians possessed and which led the way to the Gospels.

Justin's doctrine of the *Logos,* therefore, is undoubtedly a positive one, but on the matter of the third person of the Trinity, the Holy Spirit, his views were blurred and vague. We cannot really blame him for this, however, since the views of everyone else at the time were equally vague. Justin certainly realized that one of the most important functions of the Holy Spirit lay in the inspiration of the prophets, but there is no doubt that he was a little unclear about the Spirit's overall role. One of the problems here is that although the Holy Spirit is mentioned in Scripture, he, she, or it is never clearly identified, and there is a tendency in Justin's thought to confuse the functions of Son and Holy Spirit. Hermas, as we have seen, went so far as to identify them. Irenaeus of Lyons, the last person we shall consider in this chapter, is somewhat clearer on the matter, but the doctrine of the Holy Spirit would not find an even partial resolution for another two centuries, and, in any case, the main interest of these second- and third-century theologians unquestionably lay in the relationship of the Father and the Son. And as we shall see, this alone was quite sufficiently problematical.

Little is known of the life of Irenaeus (*c.* 130–*c.* 200). He was born sometime in the first half of the second century, probably in Smyrna, and was trained in Rome. From there, for reasons unknown, he made his way to Lyons (now Lyon), in the center of what is now France, where he established himself as an important and respected presbyter. In about 178 he succeeded Pothinus (who had died a martyr) as bishop, but after this he gradually becomes more and more obscure and his last years are shrouded in mystery. Even the date of his death is unknown.

The interests of Irenaeus were markedly different from those of Justin. Whereas Justin had been primarily concerned with pagans and Jews, Irenaeus was primarily concerned with the Gnostics, and this, from the start, demanded a distinct approach. It will be remembered that although the Gnostics shared certain basic convictions, they disagreed with each other on practically everything else; and it will also be remembered that a number of the sects (particularly the influential Valentinians) had no hesitation in adding a number of other gospels to those of Matthew, Mark, Luke, and John, and maintained that these apocryphal gospels contained truths too meaty for the child-like palates of the uninitiated. As a consequence of this proliferation of sources, Irenaeus realized the great importance of having an authoritative list of books which alone would be considered canonical and which could be accepted without question by all the churches. He therefore specified which books these should be (his New Testament is almost identical to that contained in the modern Bible, though he includes *The Shepherd* of Hermas and omits the Epistle to the Hebrews) and defended his choice by rational arguments.

Furthermore, he goes on, these books contain teachings handed down from the earliest times, teachings transmitted without any break from the apostles to the bishops, who were the successors of the apostles, and thence to the faithful of all the churches. 'The tradition of the Apostles which is made manifest in the whole world can be observed in every church by all who wish to see the truth.'[4] Thus,

---

4. Irenaeus of Lyons, *Adversus Haereses,* 3.3.1.

to the absurdities and disagreements of the Gnostics, Irenaeus could oppose the monolithic Church, one and holy, agreed on its canon and on the nature, order, and succession of its Apostolic Tradition. The fact that the Church was not entirely one, not entirely holy, and that the content of the canon would not finally be defined until the fourth century need not here concern us. There is no doubt that Irenaeus was on the right track.

As a theologian, Irenaeus was still a man of his times. For him, God the Father was a simple being, without parts or passions—in other words, the 'One' of Later Platonism in Christian dress—and God the Son, the Logos, is his revelation. The Holy Spirit, however, is seen in a more positive light than was the case with Justin. The Spirit is 'our communication with Christ, the pledge of incorruptibility, the strengthening of our faith, the ladder of ascent to God'.[5] And as the Holy Spirit prepares us for the Son of God, so the Son leads us to the Father, and the Father bestows upon us incorruption and immortality. And again, reflecting the Platonic subordinationism in which each rung of the ladder is lower than that above it, Irenaeus tells us that we ascend to the Son through the Spirit, and to the Father through the Son.

In other words, our redemption involves the whole Trinity just as creation involved the whole Trinity. The Son and the Holy Spirit are called the 'two hands of God', and in creating the worlds God has no need of any other helpers, assistants, angels, or gnostic *aeons*. His Word (Logos) and his Wisdom, the Son and the Spirit, were always with him, and 'through them and in them he made all things by his own free will'.[6] Then, having been brought into being by the united Trinity of God the Father and his two hands, the same united Trinity offers us the way to salvation and the joy of eternal life.

The theology of Irenaeus, then, is more distinctly trinitarian than that of Justin, though neither he nor Justin was the first to use the term 'trinity'—*trias* or 'triad' in Greek, and a word that does not appear in Scripture—for the union of the three divine persons.

5. *Ibid.,* 3.24.1.
6. *Ibid.,* 4.20.1. See also, *ibid.,* 5.1.2-3.

That honour goes to another second-century Apologist, Theophilus, bishop of Antioch. The ideas of Irenaeus, however, represent the culmination of Christian thought in the second century and we shall have cause to return to them—especially his ideas on the Incarnation and his doctrine of 'recapitulation'—in a later chapter. But for all its coherence, the theology of Irenaeus still leaves many questions unanswered. There remains a long way to go before the nature, role, and relationship of the three persons of the Trinity are clearly and unequivocally presented, and to pursue our investigations to the next stage we must return from the west to the east, from Gaul to Egypt, from Lyons to one of the greatest intellectual centres of the Roman world: Alexandria.

As we shall see in Chapter Four, Origen (*c.* 185–*c.* 254) was one of the most brilliant and original thinkers of the pre-nicene period of early Christianity. He was a theologian, biblical critic, exegete, and mystic, and is depicted here, against the towered background of a stylized Alexandria, teaching a group of male and female saints, all with haloes. Origen does not have a halo because he was never canonized. On the contrary, a number of his ideas were specifically condemned by the Church at a later date. He was, however, the most important of the rectors of the Catechetical School of Alexandria, and his influence was immense.

ORIGEN TEACHING THE SAINTS

Icon by Eileen McGuckin
Location: The Icon Studio, New York
Photo: Eileen McGuckin

IV

CHRISTIAN PLATONISM AND THE SCHOOL OF ALEXANDRIA

WE SAW in the first chapter how Christianity, despite persecution,

still managed to attract converts, and it seems that among these early

converts many were women and slaves. Indeed, Christianity seems

to have been particularly attractive to women, for it could offer a

system in which both sexes were equal before God (if not before the

members of the Christian community), in which marriage was re-

garded as a serious and binding contract, not to be undertaken lightly,

and in which sexual sins committed by a husband were, at least in

theory, as serious as those committed by a wife. In Roman society,

however, women and slaves were not, on the whole, well educated, and although the pagan opponents of Christianity over-exaggerated the point, it is true that the Christian communities of the first two centuries were not noted for their intellectual acumen.

In the early years of the third century, however, this situation began to change as more and more converts from the better-educated classes made their way into Christianity. These converts then demanded of their new faith a system of thought which would be as intellectually satisfying and as comprehensively presented as any of the other systems of the day (including Gnosticism), and they were certainly not satisfied with the undemanding pastoral writings of the Apostolic Fathers or the apologetic-oriented theology of Justin and his associates.

To respond to this demand and to provide what was needful, there came into being the Catechetical School of Alexandria. Its first known teacher was Pantaenus, a Sicilian who had converted from Stoicism. He taught in Alexandria from about 180 to his death some twenty years later, but only a few isolated fragments of his work survive. The School reached its greatest heights under the two successors of Pantaenus: Clement of Alexandria (*c.* 150–*c.* 215) and the brilliant and original Origen (*c.* 185–*c.* 254). The characteristics of Alexandrian teaching were threefold, and each of the three points follows logically from the point that precedes it. First of all, in the School of Alexandria we see the most comprehensive adaptation of Later Platonism to Christianity ever to be attempted in the Christian tradition, either before or (with very few exceptions) afterwards. Secondly, just as Platonism laid great stress on the spiritual side of things (being, as we noted earlier, an idealistic, not a materialistic, philosophy), so, too, the Christian Platonists of Alexandria were far happier when dealing with the spiritual world than with the material one. Thus, as we shall see later, they tended to stress the divinity of Christ at the expense of his humanity, and, as happened in the case of Origen, their insistence on the utter transcendence and purity of God the Father/the Platonic One could lead to exaggerated subordinationism. Thirdly, their approach to Scripture and its exegesis mirrored this other-worldly concern. They looked for the hidden and spiritual meaning of the text—the mystical meaning—rather than the literal and historical meaning, and their allegorical interpretations could lead them into rarefied heights of ethereal exegesis which are sometimes wholly splendid and sometimes plainly bizarre.

All three of these factors may be seen at work in Clement and Origen, and we may therefore turn our attention to the first of these theologians, who, born of pagan parents, probably in Athens, came to Alexandria after extensive travels and succeeded Pantaenus as head of the catechetical school sometime in the last decade of the second century.

Clement shared many of Justin's concerns, and the difference between them is a difference in degree rather than in kind. Clement still finds it necessary to defend the Christian tradition against both pagans and Gnostics, but whereas his attitude to the former is predictable (we find him opposing the superstition and immorality of many of the pagan cults with the reasonableness and moral virtue of Christianity), his approach to the latter is more interesting. He does not attack the Gnostics in the same head-on way as did Irenaeus of Lyons, but rather takes over their essential principles and reapplies them to Christianity.

What is the Gnostic claim? That they possess knowledge. Just so, says Clement, but Christianity possesses the *true* knowledge, the full knowledge of God revealed by the Divine Logos, the revelation of God, and found in Scripture and the Christian tradition. But surely the Gnostics, too, maintain that they have a secret tradition? Just so, says Clement, but the tradition of Christianity is more authoritative and more venerable: it was entrusted to the Apostles by the Son of God himself, and from them has been transmitted from father to son down to the Church of his own times. Irenaeus would have agreed. This is the 'renowned and august Rule of the Tradition'[1] which Christianity alone possesses and which comprises the true knowledge, the true *gnōsis*. Are we then saying that Christians are actually Gnostics? Yes, we are, says Clement, but there are two sorts of Gnostics: false Gnostics, who belong to one of the many Gnostic sects; and true Gnostics, who belong to the Christian Church. Christianity, therefore, is the True Gnosticism, and if

---

1. Clement of Alexandria, *Stromateis,* I.i.

it was possible for the false Gnosticism to use pagan philosophy to present a comprehensive and intellectually stimulating system, the True Gnosticism—on the principle that anything you can do we can do better—can do so as well.

Here Clement is in full agreement with Justin that God the Logos, the second person of the Trinity, is the source of all true inspiration, but he goes further than Justin in his willingness to see in philosophy a reliable and authentic preparation for the gospel. Until the Incarnation, he says, philosophy was essential to the Greeks for righteousness, but even after the Incarnation it may still prove useful in leading them to Christ. What the Law of Moses was for the Jews, philosophy was for the Greeks. Both are 'schoolteachers' or 'pedagogues' (Clement borrows the term—*paidagōgos* in Greek—from Galatians 3:24) leading their pupils directly to Christianity.

Clement, and the whole of the Alexandrian School, therefore had no hesitation in using Platonism and Stoicism to explain and interpret the Christian tradition. He himself actually refers to God the Father as 'the One',[2] adding that he is beyond form, beyond limit, beyond comprehension, and beyond description. Indeed, in his writings there are many passages where it would be difficult (unless one knew the author) to decide if one were reading the work of a Christian or a hard-line, card-carrying Platonist. The Son he refers to as Mind—the Divine Mind of Later Platonism—and this Mind became man in order to provide the human race with the most complete and perfect revelation possible, and to enable humankind to progress slowly but steadily in the knowledge of God. Nor does this progress end with death. After we have passed from this world, our sins are purged by fire (but Clement is here thinking more of the 'rational gaseous fire' of the Stoics than the straightforward flames of the Christian hell or purgatory), and we progress from mansion to mansion (and in my Father's house, said Jesus of Nazareth, there are many mansions [Jn 14:21]) to such heights and such bliss as we cannot in this world conceive.

2. *Ibid.*, V.xii.

Later generations found some of Clement's views unacceptable. As a Christian Gnostic he tended to lay too much stress on knowledge at the expense of faith, and his emphasis on knowledge led him to see ignorance as a greater evil than sin, on the premise that the sources of sin are the 'unreasonable urges' which arise from ignorance. And as for original sin, he did not accept it. How can a new-born baby have fornicated? How can that baby have fallen under Adam's curse when he or she has not yet committed a single act, much less a single sin?[3] His Platonism led him, inevitably, into subordinationism, and his Stoicism produced some very curious views about the humanity of Christ. In one passage, for example, he suggests that Christ did not really need to eat or drink since his physical body was maintained by 'holy power'. The reason he ate and drank was so that his disciples would not be led into the wrong idea that his humanity was unreal or illusory. He himself (continues Clement) was unaffected by any passions—this was the Stoic ideal—and wholly untouched by either pleasure or pain.[4] In Clement's successor, Origen, we see even more peculiarities, and despite (or because of) the brilliance and originality of many of his theories, there was scarcely one which was not the subject of later ecclesiastical censure, and scarcely any which made their way unchanged into the body of Christian tradition.

Clement was forced to flee Alexandria in about 202 as a consequence of persecution (he died, still far from Egypt, shortly before 215), and his place as head of the Catechetical School was taken by the formidable Origen. At this time he was probably no more than twenty—a brilliant, fervent, enthusiastic, and deeply committed youth—and following his appointment, he began to lead a life of strict asceticism and discipline. It was probably about this time that he interpreted Matthew 19:12 in a literal sense and castrated himself, though this story—which is transmitted by a single author, the ecclesiastical historian Eusebius of Caesarea—cannot be regarded as one-hundred-percent reliable. Origen travelled widely in subsequent years and was eventually ordained priest in Palestine in the year 230.

3. See *ibid.*, VI.ix.
4. *Ibid.*, III.xvi.

Demetrius, bishop of Alexandria, objected to this, considering the ordination to have been irregular, and deprived Origen both of his position as head of the Catechetical School and of his priesthood. He then exiled him to Caesarea, where he established another school which soon achieved great fame, and continued his literary activities unabated for a further twenty years. In 250 he was caught up in the persecution of the emperor Decius, imprisoned, and tortured. He died at Tyre, his health broken as a result of his sufferings, in about 254. He was just about seventy years old.

It is easy, as well as tempting, to spend too long on Origen. There is no doubt that he was one of the greatest and most original thinkers in the whole history of early Christianity—certainly the greatest and most original in the period before the Council of Nicaea in 325—but fascinating though his views may be, there is little point in spending a great deal of time in explaining ideas which, for a Christian, were decidedly idiosyncratic and which, for the most part, the later Church wholeheartedly condemned. We shall not linger, therefore, over his doctrine of the pre-existence of souls, or his theory of how these souls fell, or his explanation of how one of them was to become the soul of Christ, or his optimistic view that at the end of all things, all creatures, including Satan, will be redeemed and saved. His main importance for us lies in his attitude to the biblical text and its interpretation, and in one or two important comments on the nature of the Trinity which anticipate the great Trinitarian controversy of the fourth century.

Before we begin, however, a word of caution is necessary: because Origen's works were vehemently condemned and because their inordinate length made them difficult to copy, many of his writings have perished, and what survives survives, for the most part, either in fragments or in Latin translation. This introduces two problems. First, because of the nature of the fragments, it is not always clear whether Origen is setting forth a thesis to be accepted or a suggestion to be discussed. And secondly, one of his translators, Rufinus of Aquileia (c. 345–410), admired Origen tremendously and was quite prepared to 'amend' a text if he thought that by so doing he could bring it more in line with prevailing orthodox opinion. Our approach to Origen, therefore, must be tempered with caution, for we cannot always be sure that the Origen we are reading is really Origen himself.

Origen, like Clement, still found it necessary to defend Christianity (the Edicts of Toleration were still about a century away), and in his disputations with the Jews of the empire, he realized that if one were going to argue from the text of Scripture, one needed a reliable text to argue from. Both the Christian churches and the Greek synagogues of his day used a Greek translation of the Old Testament (the New Testament, of course, had been written in Greek from the start), but among the four major versions in circulation there were considerable divergences. Origen therefore produced a colossal compilation of these versions, and included with them the original Hebrew text together with its transliteration in Greek characters. And since the whole work was arranged in six columns—the Hebrew text, its transliteration, and the four Greek translations—it became known as the *Hexapla,* a word which means 'six-fold' in Greek. It survives only in fragments, and the entire work was so huge that it may never have been copied in its entirety, but it is the earliest example we have of a Christian attempt at providing a basis for scientific textual criticism.

In his attitude to the biblical text, Origen exemplifies the allegorical character of the entire School of Alexandria. Not only did this reflect the idealistic approach of Platonism, but it was also directly opposed to the views of certain semi-christian Gnostics (Marcion in particular, whom we shall meet in Chapter Seven) who held that Scripture could be understood only in a literal sense. Origen disagreed profoundly with this, and he was convinced that behind the most mundane and seemingly uninspired passages of the Old and New Testaments spiritual truths could be discerned. The literal meaning is important, Origen had no doubt of that, but it is much less important than the allegorical meaning; and a passage in, say, the book of Joshua may tell us not only about conditions in Canaan many centuries ago (this is the 'body' of the text), but also indicate something of the ideal structure of the Christian Church (this is the 'soul' of the text). Indeed, at the highest level, which is the 'spirit' of the text, it may even inform us of the nature of the relationship between the individual soul and God. Origen's so-called 'mysticism'—his delineation of the long and arduous path which leads eventually to the mystical union, or mystical marriage, between the soul and the Divine Logos—is simply a reflection and a corollary of this allegorical tendency. Origen's own soul, like the Platonic bird in its cage (an analogy we used in Chapter Two), was continually flapping its wings against the door, and given the slightest chance, the tiniest chink, it was out and off, rising from the literal world to the giddy heights of the spiritual heavens. Consequently, by beginning with an Old Testament discussion of the Israelite law of inheritance from Numbers 27, Origen can, and does, end with an account of the face-to-face vision of God, when we, too, shall become gods in Jesus Christ. This mode of exegesis had a profound and lasting effect upon the Christian tradition, and although it reached its apogee with the writers of the Middle Ages, it may still be heard, with more or less success, in the Christian pulpits of our present day.

Biblical interpretation was Origen's prime concern, and his indefatigable energy produced multitudinous commentaries of inordinate length. Yet he did not confine his talents to pure exegesis but turned them also to the preparation of the first comprehensive and systematic textbook of Christian theology. This was what the better educated and more cultured Christian converts demanded, and this was what Christianity had never previously had. The work was entitled *On First Principles* and was divided into four books. The first book dealt with celestial matters: Father, Son, and Holy Spirit, together with angels and other heavenly things; the second with earthly concerns: the world and its creation, the human race, the soul, the Incarnation, and so on; the third with psychological questions, especially free-will and its consequence; and the fourth with Scripture, its inspiration and interpretation. Despite the awkward fact that it contained numerous ideas which the Church later condemned, the volume was a remarkable achievement and provides a fascinating glimpse into the thought-world of third-century Christian Platonism. We might add that the original Greek version of the work has not survived—save for fragments, though some of these are quite extensive—and the complete work is extant only in a not entirely reliable Latin translation by Rufinus.

It is curious, however, that although Origen utilizes Platonism to an even greater extent than Clement, he also maintains that one should treat it with the utmost care. He never says, as Clement said, that philosophy is a guide to Christ, and his attitude to the philosophers, including Plato, was overtly critical. Yet no one was more deeply influenced by the ideas and outlook of Platonism, and Origen, in this matter, exemplifies the dictum 'Do as I say, not as I do'. His Platonism is clearly evident in his doctrine of the Trinity, for just as he is the most Platonic of third-century theologians, so, too, he is one of the most subordinationist. God the Father, as we would expect, is the One of Later Platonism, but although the Son/Logos is his true revelation, he is decidedly subordinate to the Father. Origen calls him a 'second god' and says, without hesitation, that although the Son and Holy Spirit excel all created things to a degree which precludes comparison since it is beyond all measure, they are themselves excelled by the Father 'by just as much or even more'.[5]

If the Father is Goodness, the Son is the image of that Goodness; if the Father is True God or God–Himself (*autotheos* in Greek), the Son is merely God; and although the Son shares with the Father an identity of will, Origen quoted with approval a statement from the Gospel of John which was to prove so embarrassing for those who later opposed subordinationism: 'The Father is greater than I' (Jn 14:28). As to the Holy Spirit, Origen appears undecided as to whether he should place the Spirit with the Creator (as the third and lowest principle of the Godhead), or with the creation (as the highest of all created things), and he is somewhat reticent about admitting its divinity. Yet for all this subordinationism, Origen introduces into his doctrine of the Trinity two concepts which were to be of first importance in events occurring a century later: the first being the principle of eternal generation, and the second the idea expressed by the term *homoousios*.

Eternal generation means that when the Father put forth or produced or generated the Son, he did not do so in the same way as a woman brings forth a baby, or a bullet comes out of a gun. In both

5. Origen, *Commentary on John*, 13.25.

these cases, the action is a *single* action, done once and for all. But when a candle shines and gives forth its light, the light is emitted continually so long as the flame is burning. It is a *continual* act, not a single action, and it is in this way that God the Son is begotten. God the Father continually pours forth God the Son, just as the rational human mind continually generates human will (this is Origen's own analogy), and since God the Father is eternal and has never been without the Son (for Origen learned from Saint John that 'he was with God in the beginning' [Jn 1:2]), so it follows that in the case of God, continual generation is *eternal* generation. From the beginning of eternity to its end, God the Father generates the Son as light forever generates its own radiance (again, the analogy is Origen's own). Light without radiance is unthinkable, says Origen, and more than that, light and its radiance show a community of substance. In other words, we have here *light* from light (the analogy is an old Platonic one), not trees from light or heat from light or horses from light. As a river puts forth a stream (water from water) or the rational mind puts forth its will (mind from mind), what is put forth here is the same 'stuff' or 'material' or 'substance' as that which puts it forth. Father and Son, light and splendour, river and stream, mind and will are each *consubstantial,* 'of the same substance', and since the Greek word for 'same' is *homos* and the Greek word for 'substance' is *ousia,* the two terms combine to form the adjective *homoousios.*

For the moment we will say no more about this important term, and whether Origen himself elaborated on it is something we do not know. Most of his writings, as we have mentioned, have come down to us only in fragments, and it is only in a fragment that this term *homoousios* is found. Indeed, it is not even certain that the word is Origen's own. Despite its appearance in a portion of his authentic writings—his commentary on the Epistle to the Hebrews—it might have been added by Rufinus, who, in ceaselessly looking after Origen's interests, may have inserted the term at a later date to improve his master's image. But whether Origen himself used it or not, there is no doubt that its appearance in the third century could not compare with its importance in the fourth, when it was introduced into the Creed of Nicaea and championed (against strong opposition) by the great Athanasius as the very watchword of orthodoxy. To this development we must now turn, for the death of Origen occurred at much the same time as the birth of Arius, who was destined to become the first of the great heresiarchs and shake the Christian Church to its very foundations.

This is how a sixteenth-century Italian painter imagined the great Council of Nicaea. Constantine is seated in the left foreground, and the Book of the Gospels is enthroned in the centre. The architecture and vestments have nothing to do with the fourth century. Mitres, for example, are not found before the eleventh century, and, in any case, Orthodox (Eastern Christian) bishops never wore them. Nebbia has painted a large number of bishops here, but fewer than the two hundred twenty or so who attended most of the sessions.

THE COUNCIL OF NICAEA (325)

Fresco by Cesare Nebbia (1534–1614)
Location: Biblioteca Apostolica Vaticana, Vatican Museums, Vatican State
Photo: Scala / Art Resource, New York

V

ARIVS AND THE COVNCIL OF NICAEA

THE EDICTS OF TOLERATION enacted between 311 and
313, whatever they might have been legally, had a profound effect
on Christianity, as we saw in Chapter One. With external persecution removed, the mind of the Church became occupied not with
survival, but with theology, and the topic which concerned it more
than any other was the relationship of Father and Son in the unity
of the Trinity. Because of the deep influence of Later Platonism,
Christian writers up to the early fourth century had all been sub-
ordinationists, but because theological thought, like all thought,
develops and progresses, ideas once acceptable were by then no
longer found to be so.

These developments came to a head in the first quarter of the fourth century when the priest in charge of one of the most important churches in Alexandria—the church of Baucalis—began to teach publicly that not only was Christ subordinate to the Father, but that 'there was, when he was not'. The priest was Arius (d. 336), a man who had been trained in Antioch in Syria, not Alexandria, and who was noted for the excellence of his preaching and the purity of his life. He had been a pupil of Lucian of Antioch, a renowned and saintly biblical scholar who was caught up in the last of the Christian persecutions and, after torture, was executed at Nicomedia in 312. Another of Lucian's students was a young man called Eusebius who (as we shall see) was to play a major role in the political and theological conflict which was just about to unfold. Arius himself moved to Alexandria at an unknown date and it was there that he was ordained priest.

But what did Arius mean by 'there was, when he was not'? Stated (for the moment) more crudely than ever Arius did, he meant that there was a 'time' when Christ the Son did not exist as a separate and distinct person of the Trinity. In the beginning there was only God the Father, who contained within himself the *potential* for the Son (we see here the clear influence of Platonic thought) and then, sometime 'later' brought the Son into being as the second person of the Trinity. There was therefore a 'time' when the second person of the Trinity had no separate reality, but existed only in potentiality in the mind of the Father. This idea was not unique to Arius, nor indeed was the phrase 'there was when he was not' (it seems to have been in circulation at the time of Origen). Theophilus of Antioch, the second-century Apologist whom we met in Chapter Three, had already distinguished between the 'immanent' Logos (the Logos in the mind of God) and the 'expressed' Logos (the Logos brought forth by and from the Father for the purposes of creation), and although the terminology might be a little complicated, the idea is simple. If I think of, say, an apple, I have the idea and image of an apple in my mind. But so long as I leave it there and do not actually utter the word 'apple', there is no communication between me and you and no-one knows what I'm thinking. But if I say 'apple' out loud, the situation immediately changes. My idea, originally tucked away in my own mind, now exists outside of myself, and by actually saying 'apple' I have, in a sense, created the concept of an apple in the minds of those who hear me. The immanent or inward apple has become the expressed or uttered apple, and there is now an essential link between me and my audience.

Arius, however, was more subtle than Theophilus, and makes it clear that all this happened before time began. Despite what I said earlier, therefore, we cannot actually say that there was a *time* when the Logos did not exist as a separate and distinct person of the Trinity, because time, as such, did not yet exist. That is why I placed the words 'time' and 'later' in quotation marks. What Arius is saying, in fact, is not that God the Father has *temporal* priority over God the Son, but that he has *causal* or *logical* priority, and it cannot be denied that he has a point. If I light a candle, the candle-flame immediately puts forth light, but although the flame does not have temporal priority over the light—the light does not appear two seconds after the flame—there is no doubt that I have to have a flame in order for the light to appear. The flame, in other words, is the cause of the light and may therefore be said to have causal priority. Arius, therefore, did not say 'there was *a time,* when he was not'—that involves temporality: 'before' and 'after', 'earlier' and 'later'—but 'there was, when he was not', and that is simply a matter of logic and causality.

For Arius, therefore, the Father was unquestionably the source of the Son (and with this the Church could not disagree), but he was equally convinced that after the Son was brought forth as the second person of the Trinity, he was unquestionably subordinate to the Father. On this point, Arius stood firmly within Christian tradition. His teacher, Lucian, had taught the same thing, and—as we have seen—it was simply the logical consequence of using later Platonic thought to elucidate the Christian idea of the Trinity. Up to this time, we might say, subordinationism was orthodoxy, and it cannot be denied that subordinationism provided answers to some very tricky questions. What questions?

According to the Scriptures, Christ did a number of things which, if he was truly and completely God, were impossible to explain. He was tempted, he 'advanced in wisdom' (Lk 2:52), he wept, he did not know the hour when the world would end, and he cried out in desperation when he was on the cross. But how can God—the infinitely perfect, omnipotent, omniscient Deity—grow in wisdom? How can he be ignorant? How can he be tempted, and so on? Surely the only way to explain these things is to say that Christ was not, in fact, God in the same sense that God the Father is God, that he was not quite perfect, not quite all-powerful, and not quite all-knowing.

Furthermore, if Christ is the mediator between God and the human race (and Scripture leaves us in no doubt on the matter), then how can he be a mediator, a 'middle-man', without being in the middle, i.e. without being something more than human but less than God? And there is still more. If the way to salvation involves the imitation of Christ (and the Church was and is convinced that this is so), how can we hope to imitate a being who is infinite in all things? If someone suggests to us that we imitate the fastest Olympic runner and try to run a hundred metres in so many seconds, we might give it a try. We might not succeed, but there is at least a remote possibility. But if someone tells us that we have to run at the speed of light and cover a hundred metres in no time at all, we would be perfectly justified in shrugging our shoulders and refusing to get changed. The thing is manifestly impossible. If, then, Christ is simply and totally God, how can we hope to imitate him? But if he is something less than God, then we might at least have a fighting chance. Subordinationism, in other words, provided neat and convincing answers to the questions of how Christ could exhibit non-divine emotions, how he could mediate between God and us, and how we could aspire to imitate him with some hope of success. It brought him within our reach.

About half a century later these questions would be answered in a different way: by insisting that in Christ there was not only the fullness of divinity, but also the fullness of humanity; and that the fullness of humanity involved true human flesh and—more importantly—a true human soul which felt human emotions and which had human limitations. But that was still in the future and, for the moment, Arius had both logic and tradition to support his case. Let us therefore return to his ideas.

According to Arius, the Son came into being by an act of the Father's will. Most theologians of his time would have agreed with him. But if the Son was brought into being by the Father, he was not uncreated (as is the Father); and if he was not uncreated, he could therefore be called 'something created' or 'a creature'. So does that mean he was no more than a creature like me or my cat? Not at all. He was created, says Arius, 'but not as one of the creatures'. Indeed not. As the Mediator, he might have been subordinate to God, yet he was certainly superior to us. Just as we must not confuse him with God the Father, so we must not confuse him with mere humanity. But as a 'creature' or 'a created thing', as something subordinate to the Father, he was not of the same substance (*ousia*) as the Father who brought him into being. If he were identical in substance to the Father, he would be what the Father is—100% God—but this, clearly in Arius' mind, is not the case. And since he was not of the same substance (*ousia*) as the Father, he was not God in the same sense in which God the Father was God. He was, in fact, God by *grace,* not by *nature.* He was God because God the Father had graciously permitted him to be God and had bestowed upon him certain attributes of divinity, but he was not God in his own right, in his own being, in his own substance.

There is no doubt, then, that Arius was subordinationist, but he might not have been quite as subordinationist as his opponents maintained. In one important matter it is possible that he was de-liberately misrepresented—one might even say framed—by those who disagreed with him. According to them, Arius not only stated that the Son was a 'creature' or 'something created', but that, like all other creatures, including the world and us in it, he had been created by God the Father out of nothing. This would indeed be an outrageous statement, and a very persuasive case has been argued by the Italian scholar Manlio Simonetti that he never did say it. It may well have been put in his mouth by his rivals to make him appear worse than he was. His later followers maintained it, that is true, but disciples are often more extreme than their master. Yet even if Arius was not as ultra-subordinationist as some maintained, subordination-ist he certainly was, and for our purposes we may summarize the essential points of his doctrine as follows: (1) there was—before time began—when God the Son did not exist as a separate and distinct person of the Trinity; (2) God the Son was created by an act of the

Father's will, but was not created 'as one of the creatures'; (3) God the Son is subordinate to God the Father for logical, traditional, and soteriological reasons; (4) God the Son is not truly God by nature—he is not *substantially* God—and, as a consequence, (5) God the Son is not of the same substance as God the Father.

The next question we must ask is why these ideas were thought to be incorrect. If this sort of thinking had developed without question for a couple of hundred years, why did it suddenly seem wrong? It is clear from the writings of Arius's opponents, particularly Athanasius the Great (whom we shall meet again), that there were three things wrong with it, and these three things are as relevant for Christianity today as they were for Christianity in the fourth century. Arian subordinationism does not work, said Athanasius, for three reasons.

First of all, Christianity has always maintained that God is, in some way, One *and Three*. This is one of the two essential features (the other is the doctrine of the Incarnation) which distinguishes Christianity from the other great monotheistic systems, Judaism and Islam, both of which assert that God is One Alone. God *is* One and Three, say the Christians, he always *was* One and Three, and always *will be* One and Three. Did Arius say this? No, he did not. According to his teaching, at the beginning of all things there was only God the Father, and then, sometime 'later' (though Arius never uses so crude a word), there came into being God the Son, and after that, the Holy Spirit. So, according to Arius, there was a time when God was not One and Three, but only One, and that (says Athanasius) is Judaism, not Christianity.

Secondly, Christianity has always maintained that worship may be offered only to God. To worship anything less than God—angels or *aeons* or pagan deities or kings or emperors or animals or anything else—is idolatry, the worship of idols. Indeed, it was in defense of this principle (as we saw in Chapter One) that so many Christian martyrs had died in so many appalling ways. But if, as Arius maintained, God the Son was subordinate to God the Father and was not truly God, then to worship Christ is to worship a being less than God, and to worship a being less than God (said Athanasius again) is not Christianity, but idolatry. And idolatry, as Saint Paul makes clear, is a very grave sin indeed.

Thirdly, Christianity maintains that salvation involves two essential principles: (1) that the iniquities of the human race have been forgiven and its many sins paid for by the death of Christ on Calvary, and (2) that this same human race is, by God's grace, permitted to share in the divine nature of Christ and to become, in a sense, divine. The New Testament says so: through the promises made to us by Christ, we 'may escape worldly corruption and become partakers of the divine nature' (2 Peter 1:4); and the theologians of the early Church had no doubt that this was true. But to redeem the whole of the human race, past, present, and future, from all its wickedness requires an infinite being who is not himself part of that race, and the only infinite being is God. Irenaeus of Lyons had said much the same thing more than a century earlier: the world cannot be redeemed by someone who is part of that world. We cannot be saved by a Saviour who is himself in need of salvation.

And as for the second point, we may summarize the principle in Athanasius's phrase: 'God became human that in him humans might become god'.[1] He did not mean by this that 'God became 70% human that in him 70% of humans might become 70% god'. In other words, if Christ was not *fully* God, not truly God, not 100% God, then (1) redemption might not be complete, and (2) the New Testament is wrong, and we are not going to share in the full divine nature, but only in a semi-divine nature, a 60% or 70% divine nature, a second best. And that, said Athanasius for a third time, is not Christianity.

Arius, we might add, was able to counter all these arguments—some of his answers are better than others—but we cannot examine the details of the controversy here. Suffice it to say that, by the time Arius was teaching his refined and subtle subordinationism, the theological wind was changing. Subordinationism had had a long and uncontested history, it is true, but by the early fourth century it was becoming clear to many theologians that although the Arian Christ offered neat answers to a number of tricky questions, there were also other answers to the same questions; and if we really were

---

1. Athanasius, *Ad Adelphium,* 4.

to become 'partakers of the divine nature', it was difficult to see how this was possible if Christ himself were not truly and substantially divine. Thus, when Alexander, the bishop of Alexandria, heard what Arius was teaching, probably sometime in 318, he ordered him to cease. Arius refused. Why should he cease? What he was teaching was what Justin and Clement and Origen had taught. It was what everyone had taught. It was Christian tradition. And it cannot be denied that Arius had a point.

Alexander, however, remained unpersuaded, and summoned a synod of Egyptian bishops to consider the matter, probably in 319. As a result of their deliberations, Arius' teaching was condemned, but Arius was not prepared to accept their decision meekly. Far from it. He strongly objected to the condemnation, and immediately sought support for himself and his doctrines among his friends in Antioch, where, it will be remembered, he had studied under Lucian. Some of those he contacted were extremely powerful, and one in particular, Eusebius (whom we mentioned above), was now bishop of the important see of Nicomedia. He was also a close friend of the imperial family and had far-reaching influence at court. It was he who would baptize Constantine on his deathbed, and there is no doubt that the emperor listened attentively to his suggestions. Furthermore, between Antioch and Alexandria there existed considerable rivalry, both political and theological, for both had Catechetical Schools and differed markedly in their outlook. Arius's appeal to his fellow Antiochenes, and the intervention of the powerful Eusebius, transformed what began as a local theological dispute into a political-geographical-theological power struggle which split the Christian world in two.

Constantine, naturally, was not pleased, and after consulting his ecclesiastical adviser, a westerner named Hosius (or Ossius), who was bishop of Cordoba in Spain, decided to send him to Alexandria to see if he could resolve the issue. Hosius, predictably, did not succeed. The conflict by now was far too intense, too political, and too violent for any such intervention to have any effect, and the situation was not helped by the fact that Hosius himself was strongly partisan and heavily biased against Arius. Constantine therefore decided to summon a council of bishops to discuss the matter, a council which would include representatives of the whole Christian world, eastern and western, and which would therefore constitute the first Ecumenical Council. His original intention was that it should meet at Ancyra (now the city of Ankara, the capital of modern Turkey), but after witnessing the underhanded operations of Hosius, who, in a number of ways, had attempted to prejudge the issue, Constantine relocated the council and commanded that it meet at Nicaea (the modern Iznik in northwest Turkey), which was conveniently situated near the imperial residence from which the emperor himself could keep an eye on the proceedings. It was also a more convenient location for the handful of western bishops who were coming to the council, and it also had a better climate.

So it was that the great Council of Nicaea convened in May-June 325 to consider, and ultimately condemn, the teachings of Arius. About two hundred-twenty bishops attended, though there may have been more at certain sessions. We cannot believe the traditional number of 318, for this was a number stolen from the book of Genesis: it was the number of Abram's servants (Genesis 14:14). Furthermore, if you translate the number 318 into Greek letters (every Greek letter is also a number), you get ΤΙΗ where Τ (tau) represents the cross and ΙΗ (*iota, eta*) are the first two letters of the name (in Greek) of ΙΗϹΟΥϹ = Iēsous = Jesus. Of the more than two hundred bishops who did attend, almost all were from the Greek-speaking east. The representatives of the west were Hosius of Cordoba, two priests who represented the pope (Silvester I, whose involvement in the great controversy was insignificant), and five other bishops. Constantine himself opened the proceedings and kept a careful eye on them throughout, but his interest was political rather than theological. What the emperor demanded was a resolution of the conflict and an end to the theological civil war which was threatening his empire.

If ever there were *acta* or minutes of the Council, they have been lost. All that survives is the letter calling the Council together, twenty miscellaneous canons or decrees dealing with a variety of subjects (e.g. the calculation of the date of Easter, the order of rank of the great metropolitan sees, certain other heresies apart from that of Arius, how one should deal with those who lapsed in the recent persecutions, matters relating to the clergy (including deaconesses), and questions of church discipline, and the very important Creed of Nicaea, of which the following is a literal translation:

> We believe in one God, Father, almighty, maker of all
> things, visible and invisible; and in one Lord Jesus
> Christ, the Son of God, begotten from the Father,
> only-begotten, that is, from the substance (*ousia*) of
> the Father, God from God, light from light, true God
> from true God, begotten not made, consubstantial
> (*homoousios*) with the Father, through whom all things
> came into being, both things in heaven and things on
> earth; who, because of us humans and because of our
> salvation, came down and became incarnate, and became
> human; he suffered and rose on the third day,
> he ascended into the heavens, and he will come to
> judge the living and the dead; and in the Holy Spirit.
> But as for those who say, 'There was, when he was
> not', and 'Before he was begotten, he was not', and
> that 'he came into existence out of nothing', or who
> allege the Son of God to be 'of a different *hypostasis* or
> substance (*ousia*)', or 'created', or 'changeable', or
> 'mutable': these the holy universal and apostolic
> Church anathematizes.

This creed, which was drawn up only after considerable discussion, was signed by all but two of the bishops at the Council. The two errant members were immediately deposed and sent home. Given Constantine's character, they got off lightly. But, in a sense, the creed is not so much a reflection of what the orthodox Christians believed as what the Arians believed and, as a consequence, what the orthodox would not accept. Look at the language: (1) the Son is *begotten* from the Father, and not, as the Arians say, created or made; (2) the Son is *true God,* and not, as the Arians say, something subordinate; and (3) the Son is of the same substance as the Father, *homoousios* or consubstantial with the Father, and not, as the Arians say, of a different substance or *ousia*. He is God from God and light from light (here is the old Platonic analogy reappearing), and not 'partly God from fully God' or 'dullness from brilliance'. And in the use of the term *homoousios* (a word, it will be remembered, which Origen may have used), the Nicene Fathers intended to imply the utter impossibility of subordinationism. How? Let us consider the question.

First, what is God the Father made of? What is his substance or *ousia*? Answer: his substance is 'divinity' or 'deity' or 'god-ness'.

Secondly, if we dig a channel from one huge lake to lead into and form another huge lake, is there any difference between the water in the two lakes? Answer: No, there is no difference. The chemical composition is the same; the wetness is the same; the colour is the same; the substance or *ousia* is the same. The water in the second lake is not 'weaker' than that in the first, nor is it less thirst-quenching, nor is there less of it. In other words, if two realities share the same substance—if they are *homoousios*—their properties are identical.

Thirdly, how does this apply to the Father and the Son? Answer: if the Father's substance is pure 'god-ness' and the substance of the Son is the same as that of the Father, then the substance of the Son is also pure 'god-ness'. And just as water is water is water, or light is light is light, or a rose is a rose is a rose, so true godness is godness is godness, and the consubstantial Son cannot be any less than, weaker than, inferior to, or subordinate to, the consubstantial Father. Two realities which share the same substance share the same powers and the same properties, and that is all there is to it. Arius and the Arians are totally wrong, and subordinationism is wholly incompatible with orthodox Christian belief.

It was these ideas which the Fathers at Nicaea (or to be more accurate, some of the Fathers at Nicaea) wished to imply by the use of the term *homoousios*. But before considering the consequences of their decision, let us take note of two other points in the Creed they drew up. First of all, notice the brevity of the clause referring to the Holy Spirit. We believe, they said, 'in the Holy Spirit as well'. And that is all they said. To learn about the Holy Spirit as lord and life-giver, who spoke through the prophets and so on, we must wait another half-century. The dispute at Nicaea was a dispute about two persons of the Trinity, not about three, and the question of the nature of the Holy Spirit still awaited discussion. In any case, as we remarked earlier, the Creed of Nicaea was not intended to be a comprehensive summary of orthodox Christian belief. We should see it more as a particular response to an emergency situation, and it answers the specific question 'Are you orthodox in what you believe about the Son of God?' It does not answer the general question 'What should an orthodox Christian believe?'

Secondly, notice the anathemas which appear at the end of the Creed. These present a neat summary of Arian doctrine (though as we have seen, Arius himself may never have claimed that the Son was created out of nothing), and they were originally an integral part of the text. But with the final defeat of Arianism in the later fourth century, they began to lose their importance, and later creeds rarely included them. Only one church—the Armenian Orthodox Church—still retains them today.

We have seen in this chapter how the views of Arius were condemned and why they were considered to be wrong. However subtly they were presented, they contained ideas which, by the early fourth century, were recognized as being incompatible with the Christian tradition. We have seen, too, how a theological dispute was transformed into a political and geographical conflict, and how the Council of Nicaea was called in an attempt to resolve the situation. And we have seen, finally, how the bishops at the Council drew up a statement of orthodox opinion on the question of the divinity of the Son, and how the term *homoousios* was intended to imply the identity of substance of Father and Son, and hence the impossibility that one could be inferior to the other. Unfortunately, this was not the only thing that the word *homoousios* could imply, and far from resolving the Arian dispute, it only exacerbated the situation and, as we shall see in our next chapter, led to problems of even greater complexity.

This unique example of an Arian baptistery dates from the period just before and after AD 500. It was built at the command of the Arian Ostrogothic king, Theodoric the Great, and lies immediately adjacent to the Arian cathedral. It is an octagonal building with a large and deep baptismal font (for total immersion), and a magnificent mosaic of the baptism of Christ in the centre of the dome. The modern ground level is considerably higher than the original, and visitors descend a number of steps to reach the main entrance (shown in the photograph).

ARIAN BAPTISTERY

Location: Ravenna, Italy
Photo: Terryl N. Kinder

VI

THE TRIUMPH OF THE NICENE FAITH

DID THE COUNCIL OF NICAEA resolve the Arian question? Of course not. People do not change their minds simply because they are told to do so, and a signature is a cheap enough way to escape the ire of an emperor. It is true that all but two of the bishops signed the Creed and thus, in theory, agreed to the condemnation of Arius and the use of the term *homoousios,* but it is also true that many of them were uncomfortable with the term and they did not all understand it in the same way. And some of them, of course, were just playing it safe under the watchful eye of Constantine.

But why were so many opposed to its use? There were three main reasons. First, because the word was not biblical. It was certainly

used by the Later Platonists, but it does not occur either in the New
Testament or in the Septuagint, the Greek translation of the Old
Testament. Was it wise, then, to place so much importance on a term
which had no scriptural—and therefore no divine—authority?

Secondly, the word had been used previously, but by people whose
opinions were highly suspect. Some of the Gnostic sects had used
it, and it had also been associated with the doctrines of a certain
Paul of Samosata, who had been consecrated bishop of Antioch
in about 260 and in 268 condemned and deposed. Paul was more
Jewish than Christian and held views far more extreme than those
of Arius. For him, God the Father and God the Son never became
truly separate and distinct—the Divine Logos was merely one of
the Father's attributes: his 'reason' or 'power'—and he saw Jesus of
Nazareth as no more than a uniquely inspired man. Paul, in fact, was
unitarian, not trinitarian, and the Church was perfectly justified in
condemning his views.

Thirdly—and this is the most important point—the word was
ambiguous. It could mean what it was intended to mean, namely,
that Father and Son *shared* the same substance. But it could also
mean something quite different, namely, that Father and Son *were*
the same substance or, in other words, the same person. And there
is a wealth of difference between saying that Arius and Athanasius
shared a common substance (i.e. 'human-ness'), and that Arius and
Athanasius were secretly the same man. It was in this second sense
(*homoousios* = same *person*) that Paul of Samosata had used the word,
and it was primarily for this reason that a large number of the bishops
at Nicaea disliked and distrusted it.

Some of them, therefore, suggested a compromise. Why not avoid
the dangerous word 'same' (*homos*) and say instead that Father and
Son are of *similar* substance? If two things are similar, they cannot
possibly be one and the same. Similarity demands duality: you cannot be similar to yourself. Furthermore, said these compromisers and
Middle-of-the-Roaders, the change in terminology is a tiny one.
In Greek the word for 'same' is *homos* and the word for 'similar' is
homoios, and if we conjoin these terms with the word for 'substance',
ousia, then there is only a difference of a single letter: *homo-ousios*
= 'of the same substance' and *homoi-ousios* = 'of similar substance'.

One of the most important of these compromisers was Cyril, bishop of Jerusalem (*c.* 315–387), who had no doubt that Christ was truly begotten from the Father, truly God by nature and not by adoption, truly co–eternal, and 'similar to his begetter in all things'.[1] But he did not like the term *homoousios* for the reasons we have already explained. *Homoiousios* was much safer.

The compromise suggestion fell on welcome ears, and many embraced it eagerly. It could so easily mean whatever you wanted it to mean. Those who were more orthodox (like Cyril) could interpret it as meaning 'The substance of Father and Son is similar [in every possible way, and the Son is the very image of the Father]'; and those who were still, at heart, more Arian (but who were not going to admit it) could interpret it as meaning 'The substance of Father and Son is similar [in a few minor ways, and we still think that the Son is an inferior being].' In other words, the great advantage and great disadvantage of the word was its breadth of meaning: we know what colour black is and we know what colour white is, but there are a thousand shades of grey.

What this meant, then, was that whereas before Nicaea there were two main parties, Arian and anti-Arian, after Nicaea there were three. The situation can be likened to a human body: to the head correspond those who were fully Nicene, who understood what the term *homoousios* was supposed to mean and who were willing and eager to use it. To the feet correspond the hard-line Arians who never did accept the term and who, like Arius himself, still thought that Father and Son were of different substance. And to the mass in the middle, from shoulders to shins, correspond those who preferred *homoiousios*—of *similar* substance—and among this very large company there were all shades of opinion as to just how similar the similarity was.

It is at this point that we must re-introduce Athanasius the Great. Born in Alexandria in about 295, he was trained in the Catechetical School of his native city, made a deacon in 319, and, as secretary, attended Alexander, the bishop of Alexandria, at the Council of Nicaea

1. Cyril of Jerusalem, *Catechesis,* 4.7.

in 325 where (even though only a deacon) he played a major role. On Alexander's death in 328, he succeeded him as bishop and, still in his early thirties, became the greatest and most outspoken defender of Nicene orthodoxy and the term *homoousios*. As a consequence he also became the greatest and most hated enemy of the Arians. The task of Athanasius was two-fold: first to oppose, then to reconcile. Thus, for some twenty years, from about 340 to 360, he opposed the Arians in every possible way. He produced a series of treatises to demonstrate where they were wrong and why they were wrong, and to set forth as clearly as possible the faith declared at Nicaea: God the Son was truly God and had never been anything less. And then, from about 360 onwards, he turned his attention to that large party of Middle-of-the-Roaders who were, on the whole, orthodox in their opinions (they acknowledged that Christ was fully God), but who preferred to use the term *homoiousios* rather than the dangerous and ambiguous *homoousios*. These he strove to reconcile and bring into the Nicene fold. He had to prove to them that *homoiousios* was even more dangerous than *homoousios* (which indeed it was: as we said, there are far too many shades of grey) and persuade them that *homoousios,* or consubstantial, was the only safe, accurate, and precise term to use: the only term which left no doubt at all about the full divinity of Father and Son, and the only term which excluded Arianism totally and completely. The extent to which he succeeded in both these endeavours is Athanasius' outstanding achievement.

His efforts, however, were not helped by circumstance, for the problems which arose after Nicaea were not only theological, but political. Indeed, there was little in the early church in which politics did not play a part, and the inspiration of the Holy Spirit was all too often mediated by intimidation and bribery. So long as Constantine was alive, the Nicene Creed remained the standard of orthodoxy, but even during that time the Arian party worked hard to recoup its losses. Its most formidable supporter was Eusebius, the bishop of Nicomedia whom we met earlier, who still had the ear of Constantine, and who, with great skill and considerable success, continually attempted to undermine the efforts of Athanasius. But after the death of Constantine in 337 the situation became utterly chaotic. Successive rulers were either pro-arian, anti-arian, or tolerant of both, and who was bishop in what diocese at what time depended almost entirely on the theological viewpoint of the reigning emperor or his advisers. Prelates moved in and out of their sees with astonishing speed, and Athanasius himself was exiled and restored to Alexandria no less than five times, spending some seventeen years in exile. This chaotic state of affairs came to an end only in 381, two years after Theodosius I became emperor. After first outlawing paganism (as we saw in Chapter One) and making Christianity the official state religion, he also decreed that Arianism should be considered a legal offence, and from the end of the fourth century it played no further significant role in the eastern Roman world. This is not to say that it was completely dead: it was a singularly hardy heresy, and after being extirpated from the centre of the empire, it took root among those who inhabited its extremities—primarily the Teutonic tribes—and flourished there for many more years. That, however, is another story and need not concern us for the present.

Throughout this half-century or so of political intrigue and party politics, Athanasius, whether in or out of exile, had been labouring assiduously on behalf of the faith of Nicaea. Again and again he had stressed the essential points: true redemption demands that Christ be true God; the Son is generated eternally from the substance of the Father; an eternal Father therefore implies an eternal Son; as the sun forever pours forth its radiance, so the light which is the Father forever pours forth the light which is the Son. But if, as Father and Son, they are two persons, yet as one God they are one substance; and if both share the same substance, both share the same power, the same glory, the same divinity, the same 'god-ness'. And how is this best expressed? Surely by the term *homoousios,* a word which demonstrates at one and the same time the full divinity of Christ, the truth of Nicaea, and the error of the Arians.

By the time of Athanasius' death on 2 May 373, Arianism was on the decline. It would be another eight years before it was finally proscribed by Theodosius, but the intense efforts of Athanasius—and certain others, as we shall see in a moment—in the fifties and sixties of the fourth century had demonstrated clearly the theological dangers of Arianism and had succeeded in luring back into the Nicene fold a great many of the Middle-of-the-Roaders. One major problem still remained: if it were true that Father and Son were one God, yet two persons, both fully divine; and if it were also true, as most now seemed prepared to accept, that the term *homoousios* best described their relationship, what about the Holy Spirit? Was it, too, fully divine? Was it, too, *homoousios*? Was it, too, truly God?

The answer of Athanasius himself was clear and logical: (1) if God is really One as well as Three, then although there may be three persons, there can only be one nature or one substance. (2) If there is only one substance for one God, then obviously all three persons must share in it. It therefore follows that (3) the third person of the Trinity, like the second person of the Trinity, must also be consubstantial/*homoousios* with the Father; and (4) if the one God is truly eternal (and no Christian would deny it), then all three consubstantial persons must likewise be truly eternal, including the Holy Spirit. Furthermore, said Athanasius, if there is but one God and not three, then when God acts, he must act as a unity. That is to say, because God is one, the Son or the Holy Spirit cannot act 'alone,' but always acts in Trinity. How? Everything is effected *from* the Father *through* the Son *in* the Holy Spirit, and we may see this principle in operation in three examples. First of all, what happened at creation? Was it not God the Father who created the worlds? No: it was GOD THE FATHER through the Son in the Holy Spirit. But surely the Incarnation was the Incarnation of God the Son, not of God the Father? True: but the Incarnation was effected from the Father THROUGH THE SON in the Holy Spirit. And at Pentecost? Who descended in tongues of fire upon the astonished disciples? God the Holy Spirit, in a dramatic action which was accomplished from the Father through the Son IN THE HOLY SPIRIT. In other words, God the Trinity is one and indivisible (the words are those of Athanasius), and although there are three distinct persons, there is but 'one operation' and 'one activity'.

The teaching of Athanasius, therefore, is that the Trinity is consubstantial, co-eternal, and co-eternally distinct in its three persons. It is also of such a nature that when it acts, it acts as a unity. And this, essentially, is also the teaching of present-day Christianity.

Athanasius, however, was in advance of his time. His view of the Holy Spirit, and therefore of the Trinity, may be what modern Christianity accepts, but it was not the view of many of his fellow priests and prelates. In 362, at a council held in Alexandria, Athanasius had managed to have accepted the proposition that the Holy Spirit was not a creature or something created, but was inseparable from the substance of Father and Son; yet at the time of his death in 373, there was still no agreement on the matter, and the question remained unresolved. Obviously something had to be done, and something was done by three remarkable theologians who flourished in the second half of the fourth century: Basil the Great (*c.* 330–379), bishop of Caesarea, an erudite and holy man with a great talent for organization; his younger brother Gregory (*c.* 335–*c.* 395), bishop of Nyssa, a man intimately acquainted with Later Platonic thought and arguably the most brilliant thinker of the period between Nicaea and Chalcedon (451); and their friend Gregory the Theologian (329–389), a learned and distinguished preacher, who was bishop of Sasima (a place he loathed) and assistant bishop to his father (also named Gregory), who held the see of Nazianzus. Since all three lived and worked in that part of modern Turkey which was once called Cappadocia, they are known collectively as the Cappadocian Fathers.

In one of the sermons of Gregory of Nazianzus we have a splendid example of the conflicting opinions about the nature of the Holy Spirit. Some people, says Gregory, think the Spirit is an 'activity' or an 'energy'. Some think it is a 'creature' or 'something created'. Some, it is true, think that it is 'God', and some just don't know what to think. And even among those who do acknowledge the Spirit's divinity, some are prepared to admit it openly, and some will only think it, finding it wiser and safer to keep their mouths shut.[2] What the Cappadocians did was put an end to this confusion and complete the work of Athanasius. The much-exiled bishop had succeeded in persuading most people to accept that Father and Son were *homoousios,* and he himself believed the same was true of the Spirit. The Cappadocians had the responsibility of getting this view generally accepted.

It was no easy task. Their main opponents were the Pneumatomachi or Pneumatomachians, a Greek word which means 'those who

2. Gregory of Nazianzus, *Oratio,* 31.5.

fight against the Spirit'. They were also referred to as Macedonians
after Macedonius (d. *c.* 362), the semi-Arian bishop of Constantinople, though there is very little evidence that he actually subscribed
to their beliefs. These 'Spirit-fighters' pointed out that nowhere in
Scripture is the Holy Spirit called 'God' (which is true), and that
in the places where the Spirit is mentioned, the clear implication is
that it is a being inferior to God. Nor could they conceive of any
relationship within the Trinity other than that of Father and Son—a
begetter and that which is begotten—and if we are to start thinking
of the Holy Spirit as the grandson of the Father, then theology has
become farcical. Against these objections, the Cappadocians moved
with determination combined with caution.

Basil, the oldest of them, began just by denying that the Spirit
is a 'creature'. He then moved on to say that it is inseparable from
Father and Son and one with the divine nature. And finally (in 375)
he asserted that the Spirit must be numbered *with,* not *below,* the
Father and the Son, and is to be accorded the same glory, honour,
and worship. But nowhere in his authentic writings do we find the
straightforward statements 'The Holy Spirit is God' or 'The Holy
Spirit is *homoousios*/consubstantial with Father and Son'.

It is Gregory of Nazianzus who takes the plunge. 'What's this?'
says his opponent, 'Is the Spirit actually God?' 'Certainly,' says Gregory. 'What's this?' says his opponent again, 'Are you saying that it's
homoousios?' 'Yes,' replies Gregory, 'if it is God'.[3] 'Furthermore', he
goes on (and here I am paraphrasing), 'don't give me this nonsense
about there being only one possible relationship in the Trinity, that
of begetter and begotten. The Holy Spirit is not created like a creature, and it is not begotten like the Son. It *proceeds,* and we know it
proceeds because Christ himself says so in the Gospel of John (Jn
15:26)!'

It is true that Gregory is not too sure of just *how* one 'proceeds'
(it is incomprehensible, he says, and we should not be so impertinent
as to pry into such matters), but then no one else was (or is) either.
But whatever 'procession' is and whatever it means, it is the distin-

3. *Ibid.,* 31.10.

guishing characteristic of the Holy Spirit: the Father is *ingenerate* (he existed and has existed forever without origin or beginning); the Son is *generated* or *begotten* (but generated or begotten eternally: we want no Arianism here); and the Holy Spirit *proceeds*. What is the difference between 'generation' and 'procession'? 'I don't know,' says Gregory, 'but there is one'.[4]

The Cappadocians succeeded in their appointed task, and the culmination of their endeavours may be seen in a council held in Constantinople in 381. It was Theodosius I who called the council, and almost two hundred bishops attended, all of them easterners. Thirty-six of them were Pneumatomachi, but finding that the theological tide was decidedly against them, they later withdrew. Yet despite the lack of western representation, the council was considered by later theologians sufficiently momentous to be termed ecumenical, and it is therefore reckoned as the Second Ecumenical Council of the universal Church. Here the Nicene faith finally triumphed. At this Council, the bishops stated formally that Father, Son, and Holy Spirit were one *ousia,* and the work of Athanasius (dead now some eight years) found its fulfilment. The Christian Church recognized a doctrine of a co-eternal and consubstantial Trinity, One and Three, and that, in its essence, has remained the accepted doctrine ever since. Fifty-six years had elapsed since the process had begun at the Council of Nicaea. Constantine had been dead for more than forty years, and Basil the Great, who had done so much to make the Council possible, had died two years before it was convened.

And Arius himself, the originator of this long and convoluted controversy? After his condemnation and deposition at Nicaea, everyone forgot about him. He lived in banishment in Illyria, on the east coast of the Adriatic Sea. But round about 336, when he was in his eighties, sick and infirm, he pleaded with Constantine to be allowed to take the sacraments before his death. Constantine agreed, and the traditional account of what then happened (which may not be correct) is best described in the words of Edward Gibbon:

4. See *ibid.,* 29.2, 39.12, 42.15 and elsewhere.

On the same day which had been fixed for the triumph of
Arius, he expired; and the strange and horrid circumstances
of his death might excite a suspicion that the orthodox
saints had contributed more efficaciously than by their
prayers to deliver the church from the most formidable of
her enemies.

And he adds the footnote:

We derive the original story from Athanasius, who expresses
some reluctance to stigmatise the memory of the dead. He
might exaggerate; but the perpetual commerce of Alexandria and Constantinople would have rendered it dangerous
to invent. Those who press the literal narrative of the death
of Arius (his bowels suddenly burst out in a privy) must
make their option between poison and miracle.[5]

5. E. Gibbon, ed. O. Smeaton, *The Decline and Fall of the Roman Empire,* 2:
285-6.

In this wholly imaginary depiction of Augustine, the saint wears magnificent vestments, with mitre, gloves, and episcopal ring, and carries the Gospel Book and a bishop's crozier. The real North African Augustine would have looked nothing like this—except perhaps for the beard—but the painting well reflects his status, prestige, and authority in Latin Christianity.

SAINT AUGUSTINE

by Piero della Francesca (c. 1420–1492)
Location: Museu Nacional de Arte Antiga, Lisbon, Portugal
Photo: Scala/Art Resource, New York

VII

THE WESTERN CONTRIBUTION

ALMOST ALL THE WRITERS and writings we have discussed so far have been Greek. The Council of Nicaea was conducted entirely in Greek and its creed and canons promulgated in Greek. Arius spoke Greek; Athanasius spoke Greek; the Cappadocians spoke Greek; and at the Second Ecumenical Council, held at Constantinople in 381, not a single westerner was present. In other words, the doctrine of the Trinity, as we have traced it so far, was almost entirely a formulation by Greek theologians. What, then, of the West? What had been going on in the Latin-speaking part of the Roman Empire while the East was aflame with Arian and anti-Arian fire? The answer to this question depends on the subject one is talking about. In the realms of ecclesiology (the doctrine of the church: what it is, what it should be, what it does) and certain aspects of sacramental theology, there were significant developments. But in the area on which we have been concentrating so far—the problems relating to the Trinity—the west contributed singularly little.

There was, certainly, Hippolytus (*c.* 170–*c.* 235), but although his most important years were spent in Rome, Hippolytus himself was an immigrant from the Greek-speaking east, and his native language (as well as the way he thought) was Greek. He was a learned and ambitious man, well versed in the philosophical systems of his day, and a voluminous writer, though much of his work has perished. His theology follows in direct line from that of Justin Martyr and the Greek Apologists. Like them, he saw the Son as the revelation of the Father, and like them, he was undoubtedly subordinationist. But in his teaching, he drew rather too clearly the line distinguishing the Father from the Son and was accused by two popes—Zephyrinus (pope from 198 to 217) and his successor Callistus (pope from 217 to 222)—of being a ditheist, someone who believes in two gods. Hippolytus, as we might expect, denied this, and, in turn, accused his accusers of failing to make any clear distinction at all between the first and second persons of the Trinity. Furthermore, said Hippolytus, Zephyrinus is a greedy, weak, uneducated simpleton, and Callistus is an ex-convict (which was true: he had been imprisoned for embezzlement, though there are grounds for thinking he was innocent), who is also guilty of moral laxity. So incensed was Hippolytus, and so great was his dislike for Callistus, that when Zephyrinus died in 217 and Callistus was chosen as his successor, Hippolytus (so we are told, but the facts of the matter are not certain) refused to acknowledge him, set himself up in opposition, and thus became the first anti-pope in Christian history. The details of this acrimonious dispute need not here concern us, and the important thing to note is that between them, Hippolytus, Zephyrinus, and Callistus were struggling with exactly the same problem as were so many of their eastern colleagues: namely, just what is the relationship of Father and Son in a united Trinity, and how do we retain the oneness of God while distinguishing the persons? Justin had used the analogy of a second torch (the Son) being lit from a first torch (the Father), but although this sort of analogy certainly clarifies the distinction between Father and Son, it is not easy to explain just how the two torches are also one.

Neither Hippolytus nor Zephyrinus nor Callistus was actually guilty of the doctrinal lapses of which he was accused. Hippolytus did not, in fact, teach that there were two gods, and neither Zephyrinus nor Callistus believed that Father and Son were the same person. What all three were trying to do was to make it clear that, although Christ the Logos was distinct from God the Father, there was still only one God, and that, although there was only one God, he was not (as Judaism maintained) One Alone. Their intentions, in other words, were honourable. What they lacked was a suitably clear terminology in which to express them.

To find such a terminology we must move from Rome to the Roman province of North Africa, where, in about 160, was born Quintus Septimius Florens Tertullianus (*c.* 160–*c.* 225), by far the most brilliant of the pre-Nicene western theologians, and the first of them to write in Latin. Tertullian was not, at heart, a philosopher: his training had been in rhetoric and law. Whether he practised as a lawyer is uncertain, but he certainly had a good grasp of legal theory and principles. But whereas Justin had thought of Socrates as a 'Christian before Christ', Tertullian regarded him simply as a corruptor of young boys. 'What has Athens to do with Jerusalem?' he asks. 'What has Plato's Academy to do with the Church?'[1] He has no time for 'Stoic Christianity' or 'Christian Platonism' and continually, time after time, lays stress on the Rule of Faith, the truth of the teaching of the Church. And what is the Rule of Faith? None other than those beliefs, immovable and immutable, set forth in Tertullian's Creed; the Rule, that is,

> of believing in one omnipotent God, the Creator of the world, and his Son Jesus Christ, born of the Virgin Mary, crucified under Pontius Pilate, on the third day raised again from the dead, received into the heavens, where now he sits at the right hand of the Father, destined to come to judge the living and the dead through the resurrection of the flesh.[2]

1. Tertullian, *De praescriptione haereticorum,* 7.
2. Tertullian, *De virginibus velandis,* 1.

It is clear from the start that we are here in a thought-world very different from that of Justin or Irenaeus or Clement or Origen—or, for that matter, Hippolytus. The philosophical principles which left so decided a mark on pre-Nicene Greek thought are here absent, and although Tertullian cannot wholly divest himself of ideas which were, after all, breathed in with every breath of air, there is no doubt that he has little time for the sometimes airy-fairy and ethereal philosophizing of his Greek contemporaries. As a man with legal training or, at least, legal interests, his approach to the Christian situation was likewise legal. We are sinners and guilty, and we stand in court before God, who is the just judge. And because he is just and because we are guilty, we are condemned and destined for damnation. Can anything be done? Indeed it can, and has been done already: Christ has paid our debt and has ransomed us; Tertullian sees in the crucifixion the central and most important feature of Christianity. We do not achieve salvation by speculating on eternal generation and the term *homoousios;* we achieve salvation within the church through the death of Christ and the blood of the Cross.

Tertullian was primarily a controversialist. He was not a systematic theologian. His violent spirit could ignite at any time, and his pen flames with ire and vituperation. He skilfully defends Christianity against the usual pagan misunderstandings; he sharply criticizes the polytheism of the Roman Empire; he vigorously attacks the Gnostics and semi-Gnostics; he utterly condemns the games and spectacles in the arenas; he viciously lambasts women who use cosmetics and jewellery and maintains that an interest in pretty clothes shows unwonted ambition and that only whores use make-up. Yet amongst all this we find long and carefully argued passages, sometimes of great originality, showing a true mastery both of Roman law and of the philosophy he affects to despise; and in two treatises in particular—one against Marcion and one against Praxeas—we find ideas and terminology which were to be of first importance for Latin Christianity.

Marcion (d. *c.* 160) was a wealthy shipowner from the Black Sea port of Sinope (now Sinop in modern Turkey), who made his way to Rome in about 140. He was also a semi-Gnostic Christian who saw a total antipathy between the God of Love preached by Jesus of Nazareth in the New Testament, and the vengeful, ignorant, and contradictory savage who dominated the Old Testament and who was worshipped by the Jews. As a consequence, since Marcion saw no relationship at all between the Old and New Dispensations, he was not prepared to admit that the Messiah prophesied by the Jews could possibly have been Jesus of Nazareth. The Old Testament and the New, the God of Law and the God of Love, the Messiah and the Christ, the Jew and the Christian have nothing whatever in common. Furthermore, according to Marcion, the only person who really understood this, who really appreciated the difference between Jewish law and Christian grace, was Paul of Tarsus. The other New Testament writers had been too much affected by their earlier Judaism. Marcion, therefore, produced an abbreviated New Testament which consisted of an expurgated version of the Gospel of Luke (which he thought was Pauline) and edited versions of ten letters of Paul (he omitted, or did not know, the letters to Timothy and Titus).

Tertullian, naturally, rejects these views, and in his five books *Against Marcion* strives to demonstrate that Marcion's views are wholly erroneous, and in direct opposition to what is correct: namely, that the God of the two testaments—Old and New—is one and the same, and that between the two testaments there is no contradiction. The one God (says Tertullian) is both just and loving; the old dispensation naturally leads to the new; and Christ is the true Messiah and the truly human incarnate Word of the one God. Tertullian was not, in fact, entirely successful in his endeavour. He had no trouble in showing that Marcion was wrong, but he had rather more difficulty in showing that Christianity was right. To prove his point he had to rely upon a considerable amount of high-flying allegorical exegesis, which was an approach that Marcion had rejected. But for all that, his treatise is an intriguing work, and is our main source of information for the ideas of Marcion himself—ideas, we might add, which were clearly popular, persuasive, and widely accepted. The Marcionites, in fact, were a real and present danger to the Church until about 190, and although their importance declined after this date, Marcionite communities were still to be found in the west until the end of the third century, and in the east until about 450.

In the case of Praxeas (*fl. c.* 200) we are once more back in the realm of Trinitarian thought. Praxeas (of whom hardly anything is known) seems to have come to Rome from somewhere in the East and arrived there towards the end of the second century, and there is no doubt that he was teaching doctrines which, though easily understood, were theologically dangerous. In his view, so far as we can reconstruct it, the three persons of the Trinity have no real and distinct existence. There was one God who, at creation, *acted* as Creator; who, in the Incarnation, *acted* as Redeemer; and who, in inspiring the prophets and apostles, *acted* as the Holy Spirit. But these successive activities lasted only so long as was needful, so that God the Son existed as a separate manifestation of the one God only so long as there was something for him to do. It is much the same with us: at one and the same time we may be parent (to a child), teacher (to a group of students), and customer (in the local supermarket). But (a) there is only one of each of us, not three; and (b) when we have finished our shopping and returned home, we are no longer a customer. These manifestations—these three ways or three modes in which we act—are limited by place and time, and if we apply the analogy to the Trinity, we see immediately that it is no Trinity at all. There is no real and eternal distinction between Father, Son, and Holy Spirit, and what we have here are not three distinct and eternal realities, but three manifestations or activities of one single reality. Hence, says Tertullian in a splendid phrase, Praxeas has thrown out the Holy Spirit and crucified the Father. For if one of my students, incensed beyond all bounds, takes out a pistol and shoots me, he shoots not only the teacher, but the customer and parent as well. Why? Because there is only one of me, not three, and the same is true of the God of Praxeas. It was for holding doctrines such as these that Hippolytus (unjustly) condemned Popes Zephyrinus and Callistus.

The ideas of Praxeas were popular, and he was certainly not the only one to hold them. They were also associated with an early third-century theologian called Sabellius, but while little is known about Praxeas, even less is known about Sabellius. We do not know when he was born or when he died, and we are not even certain where he came from. But despite that, the ideas put forth by Praxeas came to be known generally as Sabellianism. Later theologians sometimes called the same scheme Modalism, since it maintains that the three persons of the Trinity are no more than three 'modes' or activities of the one God. Sabellianism, therefore, is the direct opposite of the Logos theology of Justin. On the one hand we have Justin's analogy of two (or three) separate torches, which can too easily end up as tritheism; on the other hand we have the Modalism of Praxeas and Sabellius which can too easily end up as a variety of Judaism.

Tertullian will have none of this. He follows in the footsteps of theologians like Irenaeus of Lyons and maintains, first, that God was *always* three and one, and that the three distinct realities of Father, Son, and Holy Spirit were *always* three distinct realities. Secondly, he maintains that in the unfolding of the divine plan—creation, incarnation, redemption, Pentecost—each of these three realities is revealed separately and fully. In the incarnation, therefore, it is not just the one God 'acting' as Christ, but the truly distinct and eternal Son of God revealing himself in flesh at this moment in time. And by what name may we refer to these three realities? Here Tertullian takes advantage of the precision of Latin (we have seen all too much of the ambiguity of Greek) and establishes a terminology which was henceforth to be accepted as the standard terminology of the western Church: there are three persons (*personae*) in one substance (*substantia*), and there is one God and one Trinity (*trinitas:* he is the first to use the Latin word in this context).

These terms are not ambiguous. 'Person' can never mean 'substance', and 'substance' can never mean 'person'. But as we have seen, the same was not true of the word *ousia* in Greek. It could mean either, which is why *homoousios* could imply 'same person' as well as 'same substance'. But if we maintain that Father, Son, and Holy Spirit are all the same *person,* we are back with the heresy of Praxeas and Sabellius. It was not until the time of the Cappadocian Fathers that Greek terminology became equally unambiguous, and we might say with some truth that if the Fathers at Nicaea had spoken in Latin and used the word 'consubstantial' rather than *homoousios,* the work of Athanasius might have been reduced by half. It is no accident that in these pages I have used the terms 'substance' and 'person' throughout, even when speaking of the Greek east before such clarification existed. But without such unambiguous terminology, borrowed with thanks from Tertullian, any description of the complexities of the Arian crisis would become even more confusing than it already is.

Tertullian's contribution to trinitarian doctrine was, however, primarily terminological. His understanding of the trinitarian relationships reflected the ideas of his times and his sources, and he was, as we might expect, subordinationist. Although he recognizes that Father and Son share a common substance, he still believes they are different in degree. If the Father is the whole substance, the Son is only an outflow or derivation (*derivatio* in Latin), or a part or portion (*portio* in Latin), of the whole. 'The Father', he says, 'is different from the Son because he is greater, just as the one who begets is different from the one begotten, or the sender from the one who is sent.'[3] But this, as we have seen, is standard pre-Nicene thinking, and we would hardly expect anything else.

Tertullian ended his days outside—or on the fringes—of orthodoxy. In 207 he joined an apocalyptic movement known as Montanism. It had been founded by an obscure figure called Montanus (hence the name), and combined extremely rigorous ascetic demands with a belief in charismatic prophecy and the imminent arrival on earth of the Heavenly Jerusalem. According to Montanus, the celestial city was due to descend at any moment near Pepuza in what is now western Turkey. It was as a member of this movement that Tertullian died, sometime after 220, although the precise year of his death is not known. His contribution to western Christianity was considerable, not only for the terminology which he provided, but also for the way in which he stamped it with a distinctive character. His legalistic approach to the tradition, his stress on the Rule of Faith, his distrust—at least in theory—of philosophy, his emphasis on belief rather than speculation: all these appear clearly in Tertullian, and he is generally considered as one of the two outstanding Latin Christian writers of the patristic period. The other is the titan figure of Augustine of Hippo.

Tertullian's death came about a century before the Council of Nicaea, but despite the fact that, thanks to him, western theologians had the necessary terminology to talk about the Trinity, they seemed disinclined to do so. There is no doubt that at the time the Arian controversy was raging in the east, many of the western bishops had

3. Tertullian, *Adversus Praxean*, 9.

only the vaguest understanding of what the fracas was all about and a large number of them never saw a copy of the Nicene Creed until years after the council. Many of them believed what it was politic for them to believe (we saw in the last chapter how chaotic were the events after 325); but in the years following Nicaea, as the Greek east slowly but inexorably leaned more and more towards the ideas of Athanasius, it pulled the Latin west along with it. To this tendency Athanasius himself made some contribution—many years of his various exiles were spent in the west—and so, too, did the remarkable Hilary (c. 315–67), a convert from Later Platonism, who became in due course bishop of Poitiers in what is now central France.

Hilary was a man at home in two worlds. He was fluent in both Greek and Latin, and just as familiar with eastern ideas as with western ones. He became the leading Latin theologian of his day, and for his unwavering opposition to Arianism and his defence of the faith of Nicaea, he is often referred to as the 'Athanasius of the West'. Partly as a consequence of Hilary's efforts, partly as a consequence of the political situation, and partly as a consequence of the natural flow of ideas, western trinitarian thought in the post-Nicene period reflected that of the east; and after the Council of Constantinople in 381—the Second Ecumenical Council—the vast majority of Christians, of whatever language and country, were prepared to acknowledge a consubstantial and co-eternal Trinity in which all three persons were co-eternally distinct, yet operated together as a unity.

The momentous and unique contribution which the west was to make to this doctrine would not occur until the early years of the following century, when Augustine of Hippo developed what is known in technical theological jargon as the doctrine of the Double Procession of the Holy Spirit.

Augustine was born at Tagaste, in the Roman province of North Africa, in 354. His father was pagan, but his mother was deeply christian and Augustine's early education was likewise christian. He had originally intended to become a lawyer, but this ambition seems to have faded fairly rapidly, and from 373 his main interest lay in philosophy. Shortly after 373 he became a Manichaean. This was a dualistic semi-gnostic system, having its origins in Persia, which Augustine embraced for more than a decade, but which he eventually abandoned

when it was manifestly unable to answer a number of fundamental
questions which had been troubling him for years. He then moved to
Rome, and from Rome to Milan, where he adopted the principles of
Later Platonism and came under the influence of the learned bishop of
Milan, Ambrose (c. 339–397). It was Ambrose who acted as the catalyst
in Augustine's conversion, and in 387, at Easter, he was baptized. The
next year he returned to North Africa, where he was ordained priest
in 391, and from then on his influence and importance in the African
Church increased rapidly and dramatically. In 396 he was consecrated
assistant bishop of Hippo, and from the following year to his death in
430 he governed the diocese as sole bishop.

Augustine's impact on western Christian thought was immense—
for many centuries, the terms Western Christianity and Augustinian
Christianity were simple synonyms—and in due course we shall be
examining his ideas on sin, salvation, the Church, and the sacraments.
For the moment, however, our concern is with the Trinity, and as
we said earlier, our immediate interest is the Augustinian doctrine
of the Double Procession of the Holy Spirit, a doctrine which was
to have wide–reaching political as well as theological ramifications
and which was to establish a permanent distinction between the ways
in which the east and the west viewed the threefold nature of God.
What, then, is this doctrine, and how did it come about?

Perhaps the best way to appreciate it is by using some simple
analogies: like all analogies, they cannot be pushed too far, but they
may help us to understand what is going on. Up to the time of
Augustine—up to the early fifth century, that is—both east and
west had a very similar idea of the way in which the Holy Spirit
was produced: it proceeded (this, we may remember, is the official
New Testament/Cappadocian term) *from* the Father *through* the
Son. Tertullian illustrates this by using the analogy of a spring (=
the Father) producing a river (= the Son), and a canal (= the Holy
Spirit) being led off from the river; and if we take over this analogy
and update it, we can visualize the Father as an infinite reservoir of
water, the Holy Spirit as the tap at which we drink, and the Son as
the system of pipes and channels linking the two together. Or, if you
prefer, the Holy Spirit is the electric socket in the wall; the Father
is the power station; and the Son is the grid-system connecting the

one with the other. In all these cases the third principle is chan-
nelled *through* the second principle *from* the first principle, and the
theory is therefore referred to as *Single* Procession, since the Holy
Spirit proceeds from the Father alone, and the Son merely does the
'channelling' or 'mediating' or 'transmitting'.

Now sometimes, when water travels through a series of pipes, it
picks up certain chemicals or other materials from the pipes themselves. Thus, when we turn on the tap and fill up a glass, we get not
only the pure water from the reservoir, but pure water *plus* the various additions which it has accumulated during its travels. Similarly,
a number of theologians (Gregory of Nyssa was one) maintained
that the Spirit 'received from the Son' during the procession. Just
what the Spirit received is not made clear, but what Gregory and
the others wanted to imply was that in the process of the production of the Spirit, the Son was not just a passive agent, but did, in
some wondrous way, make a positive contribution to the nature of
the third person of the Trinity. Yet for all this, the eastern theologians—and those in the west up to the time of Augustine—remained
loyal to the concept of Single Procession and to the two important
prepositions *from* and *through*.

Augustine's view of the Holy Spirit is radically different, and we
must use a radically different analogy to explain it. Expressing it in
human terms, Augustine says that the Father eternally generates
the Son, and that the Holy Spirit is not something which comes
from the Father alone, but is the mutual love which Father and Son
have for each other. In fact, he goes further than this, and says that
the Holy Spirit is 'whatever is common' to Father and Son—their
mutual love, for example, or their mutual joy, mutual peace, mutual
will, mutual happiness, mutual blessedness, mutual goodness, mutual
charity, mutual delight, and anything else of this nature we care to
name. But the problem with the human analogy is that we tend
to think of fathers and sons as real and solid beings, and love as an
amorphous and emotional warm fuzzy something which is 'made' or
'fallen into'. So a better analogy, perhaps, is that of an electric battery.
Here we have *forces,* not people, and we can visualize the Father as
the positive pole, the Son as the negative pole, and the Holy Spirit
as the current flowing and flashing between them. Here we have

only one substance (electricity), and if the battery is to work, all three realities must be present and operating. You can no more get a current from a battery with one pole than you can lift yourself up by your own shoelaces. In the production of the electric current, both poles are essential, and both have an *equal* part to play. To think of an eight-volt battery in which the positive pole produces seven volts and the negative produces one is ridiculous: the whole battery produces eight volts, and the two poles cooperate to precisely the same extent in producing the current.

This, essentially, is how Augustine thought of the Holy Spirit. The infinite power which is the Father generates eternally the infinite power which is the Son (so they are consubstantial and co-eternal), and these two infinite powers eternally interact to produce the third infinite power which is the Holy Spirit. In other words, Augustine is not thinking of the procession of the Holy Spirit like this:

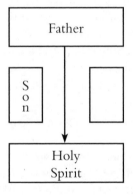

But like this:

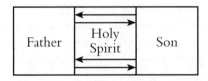

And since in this second scheme both Father and Son make *equal* contributions to the production of the Holy Spirit—the one is just as important as the other—the doctrine is referred to as *Double* Procession. Here the Holy Spirit proceeds not from the Father *through* the Son, but from the Father *and* the Son, and (as we said above) in later centuries this concept was to have profound political as well as theological consequences.

From the time of Augustine onwards the western Church accepted this doctrine (and still does); the eastern Church did not (and still doesn't). But both Churches recognized a Trinity in which all three persons were consubstantial, *homoousios,* co-eternal, co-eternally distinct, and which operated as a unity. Since it was the three Cappadocian Fathers who finally managed to get this view accepted, we may refer to it as 'Cappadocian orthodoxy'. So from the end of the fourth century, the eastern churches have had a doctrine of the Trinity which can be summarized as 'Cappadocian orthodoxy with Single Procession', and since the time of Augustine the western churches have had a doctrine of 'Cappadocian orthodoxy with Double Procession'. And that—more or less—is how it has remained ever since.

The white-bearded bishop depicted here is Gregory of Nazianzus (329/330–389/390), one of the three Cappadocian Fathers. He was usually called Gregory the Theologian, and that is the name that appears on the right of the icon. He was the son of the bishop of Nazianzus in what is now modern Turkey, and began his religious life as a monk. He was then pressured into becoming a priest, and *c.* 372 was consecrated bishop of Sasima. He never lived there, however, and stayed in Nazianzus as assistant bishop to his father, who died in 374. In 379 he was summoned to Constantinople and played an important role in the Second Ecumenical Council in 381. In the course of the council he was appointed patriarch of Constantinople, but resigned the position before the end of the year. He died in retirement about eight years later.

GREGORY THE THEOLOGIAN

Icon by Eileen McGuckin
Location: The Icon Studio, New York
Photo: Eileen McGuckin

VIII

CHRIST: BODY AND SOUL

BY THE END OF THE FOURTH CENTURY the Christian world was either convinced, or well on its way to being convinced, that Christ the divine Logos, the second person of the Trinity, was truly God. But what happened when this divine Logos became incarnate? How did the Godhead combine or conjoin or unite with the manhood in the single person of Jesus of Nazareth? Was he a man in whom God dwelt? Or was he merely a man inspired by God? Or was he a man who *was* God? What was it that Mary bore?

To answer these questions we must first travel back in time from the Cappadocian Fathers to the Apostolic Fathers, and look at what they had to say on the matter. Their concern lay almost entirely with demonstrating the *reality* of Christ's incarnation—that he was real flesh and blood and bone and sinew—for there was a pronounced tendency among some Christian (particularly Gnostic and semi-Gnostic Christian) communities of that time to deny this and maintain instead that Christ only *appeared* to be human. At the root of this idea lurked Later Platonism with its hierarchy of being. As we pointed out in Chapter Two, the view of the Platonists was that the further down the scale you descended—from the One to the Divine Mind to the World-Soul to the world—the worse things became, and this conception had been exaggerated by the Gnostic sects, who, by interposing large numbers of *aeons* or intermediaries between the Source of All Things and this world, had utterly removed the one from the other, and saw created stuff—rock, flesh, wood, blood, what have you—as straightforwardly evil. For these Gnostics and Platonic Christians, there was very little (if anything) good about flesh and bone, and they were quite unable to understand how a truly good being—i.e., Christ the Logos—could possibly be united with something truly bad or imperfect—i.e. human flesh. It would be like saying that white could be black or a square could be a circle. The thing was manifestly impossible.

Their solution to the problem was simple: Christ did not *become* man, but only *appeared* to be a man. His humanity was an illusion, an appearance: his disciples and everyone else thought he was real, but this was not the case. They were like the audience in a 3-D movie, mistaking the figure on the screen for a real person, responding to him, talking to him, learning from him, and failing to realize that what they took for reality was not reality at all, but simply an ever-changing pattern of beams of light. And since the Greek word for 'appearance' was *doketos,* this view became known as docetism, or 'appearance-ism'. As we saw in Chapter Four, Clement of Alexandria's opinion was dangerously close to this position.

To this idea, the Apostolic Fathers (together with the Apologists and their successors) objected in the strongest terms. And quite rightly. Docetism spells disaster for Christianity, and an unreal Saviour can only produce an unreal salvation. If Christ's humanity was an illusion, his suffering and death on Calvary were an illusion. If his suffering and death were an illusion, his resurrection was an illusion.

And if his humanity, suffering, death, and resurrection were all an illusion, the redemption of the human race was also an illusion. In other words, if Christ's flesh were not true flesh, then we are still in our sins. 'If these things were done by our Lord only in appearance', wrote Ignatius of Antioch, 'then my chains are only an appearance',[1] and he advised his readers to have nothing to do with anyone who avoided speaking of Jesus Christ of the line of David, who was truly born of Mary, who truly ate and drank, who truly suffered under Pontius Pilate, who truly died, and who was truly raised from the dead by God the Father.[2]

For many of the Gnostics, however, this insistence on the reality of Christ's humanity was not of any great consequence. Their view of the matter was that salvation was achieved by knowledge, not by the crucifixion, and their Christ was a Christ who revealed names and passwords and Gnostic truth, not a Christ who came to die. It made no difference to them, therefore, whether Christ was truly human or not, just as it makes no difference to us whether we are taught, say, geography by a human teacher in the classroom or by a videotape at home. But this was never the orthodox Christian view. For orthodox Christians, Christ died for our sins—Saint Paul is quite clear on the matter—and you cannot kill a videotape.

As a consequence of such arguments as these, and as a consequence of the decay of Gnosticism in the course of the third century, docetism gradually became less and less important, and by the end of the pre-Nicene period it was generally accepted among Christians that the flesh and blood and sufferings of Jesus of Nazareth were real flesh and blood and sufferings, and that the salvation of humanity could only be achieved by a truly human saviour. But if Jesus' flesh was indeed true flesh, how was it animated? What made it work and walk and talk? In ordinary human beings it was the soul which was seen as the animating agent, and the Christian world defined death simply as the separation of soul and body. The most obvious suggestion, therefore, was that just as an ordinary human being is flesh and

1. Ignatius of Antioch, *To the Smyrnaeans,* 4.2.
2. Ignatius of Antioch, *To the Trallians,* 9.1-2.

blood animated by a rational soul, the incarnate Christ was flesh and
blood animated by God the Son, the second person of the Trinity. It
is just like slipping a letter into an envelope, or filling a bottle with
wine, or wrapping a candy in paper. You take the body born of Mary
on the one hand and Christ the Logos on the other, slip the latter into
the former, and lo and behold! we have the incarnate Christ in the
person of Jesus of Nazareth. And it was this simple and straightforward
way of regarding the incarnation which dominated Christian thought
from its beginnings to some fifty years after the Council of Nicaea.
In theological jargon, it is referred to as Word-Flesh Christology: i.e.
the belief that in Christ there is only the Divine Word and human
flesh. There is no human soul.

Enter Apollinaris, bishop of Laodicea. Born about 310, he became
in due course a close friend of Athanasius and a staunch defender of
the faith of Nicaea. He was consecrated bishop of Laodicea (a city
on the coast of present-day Syria, just opposite Cyprus) in about
360, and as an orthodox bishop of an important diocese, Apollinaris
(or Apollinarius, as he is also called) was in no doubt that Christ the
Logos was truly God and truly divine, and that when he became
incarnate, his flesh was truly real and truly human. So far so good.
But it was Apollinaris's staunch support for the faith of Nicaea—including the all-important word *homoousios*—which was to cause
problems. He (like Athanasius) was convinced that only the infinite
and perfect Logos, who was not himself part of creation, could save
creation; and he was equally convinced that if the Logos was truly
and completely God (and that is what the term *homoousios* implied),
then he could not display any ungodlike characteristics. Apollinaris
was determined to keep the second person of the Trinity on exactly
the level of the Trinity, and he would have nothing to do with any
idea which seemed to bring him down to the human level.

In Apollinaris' opinion, therefore, Christ did not have a human
soul. To have one would be manifestly impossible. If, in Christ, there
was a human soul as well as the divine Logos, then (1) we would
make Christ into a sort of schizophrenic or a dual personality, and
(2) we would be maintaining that in God incarnate there existed the
possibility of sin and moral progress. It is, after all, the human soul of
a human being which (through the medium of the body) feels pain,

develops morally, and faces temptation. This can easily be proved by sticking a pin in a corpse or inviting it to have a drink or a cigar. What happens? Nothing. It is not the flesh—the meat—which feels pain and temptation, but the flesh animated by a rational soul, and Apollinaris was not prepared to admit that there was such a soul in Christ. Christ was the incarnate *God,* consubstantial with the Father, and God cannot feel pain, cannot be tempted, and obviously does not make moral progress. Christ, said Apollinaris, is 'God enfleshed' or 'God bearing flesh' (they are some of his favourite terms), and in Jesus of Nazareth there is neither need nor place for a human soul.

Furthermore, said Apollinaris, as a result of this intimate fusion of the divine Logos and human flesh, the nature of the flesh is to some extent transformed. Christ, after all, is not two beings—Logos and flesh—but one. Apollinaris was no dualist, and he insisted on the absolute unity of Godhead and flesh in the one person of Jesus of Nazareth. There is, he said, 'one nature of the Word of God enfleshed', and so intimate is the union that the properties of divinity are communicated, to some extent, to the flesh with which it is united. To use the analogy we used earlier: if you write a letter on perfumed paper and then slip it into an envelope, the envelope will absorb the scent and itself become perfumed. In just the same way, the flesh of Christ became 'divine flesh' or 'God's flesh', and therefore capable of certain actions which are not normally possible for ordinary human beings. It could walk on water, for example, or be transfigured, or survive death. And Apollinaris took these ideas to their logical conclusion by maintaining that in the eucharist, too, the bread becomes not just the flesh, but the *divine* flesh of Christ, and that when believers partake of this bread/flesh, they are 'deified' or 'divinized' by doing so. Christ's flesh, imbued with the divine powers of God the Logos, actually communicates divinity to those who consume it.

We might add that this idea of 'divine flesh' was not always understood correctly. Some of the opponents of Apollinaris thought that he was maintaining that Christ's flesh had actually been created for him in heaven—a sort of pre-existent flesh—and that he brought it down to earth with him when he was born of Mary, but this was never Apollinaris's teaching. What he said might have been theologically dubious, but it was not that dubious.

As we have seen, this concept of the incarnation—Word-Flesh Christology—had a long previous history. Apollinaris develops the idea further than his predecessors, that is true, but there is no doubt that he was building on a well-established tradition. Unfortunately, as we have seen before (most notably in the case of Arius), ideas which were acceptable at one time may not be acceptable at another, and the views of Apollinaris, which might have caused no comment half a century earlier, became the target of determined attack in the late fourth century by those energetic and capable defenders of orthodoxy, the Cappadocian Fathers. They had three main objections to the views of Apollinaris.

First, if the flesh of Christ is 'divine flesh', then it is not ordinary human flesh; and if it is not ordinary human flesh, then what is it? It is an easy step to say, 'No, it isn't ordinary human flesh; it only *appears* to be so.' But if we say that, we teeter on the brink of Docetism, and by this time it was well known that docetism was not a viable Christian alternative.

Secondly, just what is a real human being? Surely, said the Christians (and almost everyone else west of India), a human being is body plus soul, and the truly human thing about a truly human being is not the meat and muscle—birds and animals have that—but the rational human soul. Furthermore, there is a wealth of evidence in the New Testament which shows that Christ *was* subject to human emotions and passions—he got angry, he was sad, he rejoiced, he wept, he was thirsty—and since God the Logos is, by definition, exempt from feelings and emotions, and since human flesh, dead or unanimated, is good for nothing (even eating it is considered bad form), then the only thing that could possibly feel these emotions is the human soul. In other words, if we believe that Christ was truly human, and if we believe the New Testament, then we must also believe that a human soul was an integral part of his constitution. In any case, says Gregory of Nazianzus, what could be clearer evidence than the agony in the garden of Gethsemane? Here we have a superb example of conflict between the human soul and the divine Logos: 'Father, let this cup pass from me', says the human soul; 'but your will be done', says the divine Logos (Lk 22:42). And so great was the agony, say some versions of Luke, that his sweat became mixed with blood.

The third argument is the most important, but it is also the most theological, and to understand it we must go back in time to the letters of Paul and the writings of the apologist Irenaeus of Lyons. According to Paul, 'just as in Adam all die, so also in Christ shall all be made alive' (1 Cor 15:22), and later in the same letter he contrasts the first Adam—Adam—with the second or last Adam—Christ (1 Cor 15:45-50). This parallelism is much elaborated by Irenaeus (though the process started with Justin) in a doctrine conveniently referred to as 'recapitulation', a word which means literally 'summing up all previous events', Irenaeus contrasts the first Adam and all that he did with the second Adam and all that he did, and shows how the obedience, sinlessness, and perfection of the second Adam (= Christ) has cancelled out the disobedience, sinfulness, and imperfection of the first Adam (= Adam), and that in the incarnation we therefore see the beginning of the new and restored creation. It is just like the two pans of a balance: in the left-hand pan we put Adam; in the right-hand pan, Christ. In the left, Adam's disobedience; in the right, Christ's obedience. In the left, Adam's sin; in the right, Christ's sinlessness. And so on. Everything we put in one pan must be counter-balanced by what goes in the other, for everything which went wrong in Adam has been put right in Christ.

It is this doctrine which forms the basis for the arguments of the Cappadocians, and three essential points follow from it.

First of all, Christ, in the right-hand pan, must balance Adam in the left. But of what did Adam consist? Unquestionably, he consisted of body *and soul*. Therefore, if one pan is to balance the other, Christ must also have a body *and soul*.

Second, if Adam was truly tempted and fell, Christ must also have been truly tempted, yet did not fall. But as we explained earlier, the unchangeable God cannot be tempted, and you cannot tempt inanimate flesh. It is the *human soul* which is tempted and which uses the flesh to satisfy these temptations. If, then, Christ was really tempted (and Matthew 4:1 says that he was: 'Then Jesus was led into the desert by the Spirit to be tempted by the Devil'), he must have had a temptable soul. But if, on the other hand, he was *not* really tempted (and the divine Christ of Apollinaris is, essentially, untemptable), then he could claim no credit for not having fallen, and we have put nothing in the right-hand pan of the balance to cancel out what we have put in the left. My cat, for example, has been castrated, and therefore gains no credit for living a disciplined, quiet, sober, and celibate life.

Third, the sin of Adam affected not only his body—which became mortal, and subject to death, disease, and corruption—but also his soul, which developed a tendency to wickedness and became stained and tainted with sin. All humanity, therefore, has contracted these problems, and all humanity has been corrupted in both soul and body. It follows, then, that if we are to be redeemed fully, we must be redeemed in both soul and body, and for that to occur, both soul and body must have been present in Christ. As Adam's body became subject to death, Christ's body triumphed over death; and as we died in Adam, so we shall live in Christ. As Adam's soul became stained with sin, Christ's soul was pure and sinless, and in and through Christ we are offered forgiveness of sins and everlasting life. But as Gregory of Nazianzus said: 'What was not assumed was not restored'.[3] If Christ did not assume true flesh, our flesh has not been redeemed; if he did not assume a true human soul, then our souls, and therefore we, are still in our sins. Half a redemption is no good to anyone.

There are, in fact, certain problems with this doctrine of recapitulation. The most obvious is that if Adam = body + soul, but Christ = body + soul + Logos, there is already an imbalance. But there seems little doubt that the arguments and efforts of the Cappadocians met with great success and wide acceptance. They were not the first to voice their suspicions of Apollinaris's theories (the same or very similar views had already been condemned at a council held in Alexandria in 362), but the prestige, authority, and theological skill of the Cappadocians ensured that its downfall was more rapid and more complete. Apollinarianism was condemned at a series of councils (including the Second Ecumenical Council) held between 378 and 381, and then, in a number of decrees issued between 383 and 388, Theodosius I, the emperor who had already outlawed Arianism, also placed Apollinarianism beyond the pale of the law. By this time,

3. Gregory of Nazianzus, *Epistola,* 110.7, and elsewhere.

however, Apollinaris himself had left the Church, but of his later years nothing is known and he died in obscurity in about 390.

We may say, then, (1) that by the end of the third century Docetism was generally recognized to be unacceptable, and the majority of orthodox Christians were agreed that the flesh of Christ was real; and (2) that by the end of the fourth century, Apollinarianism had been condemned and the majority of orthodox Christians were agreed that he also had a real human soul. This later Christology is referred to as Word-Man Christology, for a man is, by definition, a male human being with a rational, human soul. The question which must now engage our attention is just how this true humanity, body and soul, was united with the true divinity, and precisely what terminology was best suited to express it. To deal with this we must move on in time from the fourth century to the fifth, take a deep breath, and immerse ourselves in one of the most complex and confusing controversies ever to trouble the Christian world.

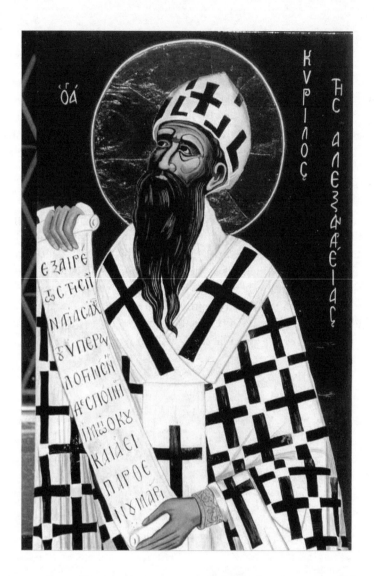

Here we see an icon of the formidable adversary of Nestorius, patriarch of Constantinople. His name 'Saint Cyril of Alexandria' (d. 444) appears in Greek to the left and right of his halo, and he is dressed in the robes of an eastern bishop. He is also bearded, as were all eastern and most western clergy at this time. Cyril was a brilliant theologian, though not always entirely ethical when it came to ecclesiastical politics. Against the views of Nestorius, he championed the use of the title *Theotokos* or 'God-bearer' for the Virgin Mary, and his devotion to the Mother of God is expressed in the scroll he holds in his hands. There, in Greek, Mary is extolled as all-holy, pure, blessed, glorious, and ever-virgin.

CYRIL OF ALEXANDRIA

Icon by Eileen McGuckin
Location: The Icon Studio, New York
Photo: Eileen McGuckin

IX

CHRIST: GOD AND MAN

TO UNDERSTAND MORE EASILY just what was going on in the great christological controversy it will be helpful if we make three preliminary points. They are, in fact, fundamental for appreciating the theological, political, and personal problems which lay at the root of the conflict.

The first point involves the distinction between *confusion* of natures and *separation* of natures, for these represent the two unacceptable extremes between which we must steer a difficult middle course. By 'natures' we mean the two natures which were united in the single person of Jesus of Nazareth: the nature of the Godhead (= the second person of the Trinity, God the Logos, consubstantial and co-eternal with the Father and Holy Spirit) and the nature of the manhood (= the flesh born of Mary, animated by a rational human soul). In other words, the two natures are the full and perfect divinity on the one hand, and the full and perfect humanity on the other.

What, then, do we mean by 'confusion' of these two natures, and why is it unacceptable? As usual, an analogy may be useful. Let us symbolize the divinity by whisky and the humanity by water and mix them together. The result? Whisky-and-water: a drink in which the non-alcoholic nature of the water has been made alcoholic by the admixture of the whisky, and the strength of the whisky has been diluted by the admixture of the water (though this is not a part of the analogy I wish to stress). Furthermore, once the two are mixed together, it is impossible to separate them (we are in a bar, not a laboratory), and again, since the whole of the liquid is now alcoholic, we may easily make the mistake of attributing to the whisky the properties of water and to the water the properties of whisky, thus imperilling the entire Scottish economy.

Let us now apply this analogy to the incarnation. If the divinity and humanity are mixed in this way, the humanity is transformed (the water becomes alcoholic) and thereby loses its true nature. It is no longer human as we are human, and a non-human or not-quite-human Saviour cannot save the human race. Furthermore, as a consequence of the fusion we may be led to assert of divinity what should only be asserted of humanity, and of humanity what should only be asserted of divinity. We may thus be tempted to speak of an eternal man or a weeping Godhead, or to suggest that when Christ, on the cross, cried out, 'My God, my God, why have you forsaken me?' he was talking to himself. 'Confusion of natures', therefore, or 'confused union' leads to a denial of Christ's human-ness and to the theologically unacceptable position that God the Logos felt pain, or that the second person of the Trinity, the immutable and unchangeable Wisdom of God, grew in wisdom (Luke 2:40). Such an idea cannot be accommodated within the Christian tradition. God has neither parts nor passions, and the theologians of the early Church knew from the letter of Saint James that in God there is neither change nor variation (James 1:17).

What, then, of 'separation' of natures? Here we go to the opposite extreme and maintain that no real union has taken place at all. In this case we may symbolize the divinity by a block of black ebony and the humanity by a block of light pine: we place one block on top of the other, and that is all there is to it. There is certainly no confusion here—you can see the dark wood and the light wood without the slightest difficulty—but neither is there any uniting. One block is just resting on the other (it is not even glued to it) and may be removed at any time. If we now apply this to the incarnation, we see that Christ is not 'the God-man'—a true union of divinity and humanity—but 'God-with-man' or 'God-resting-on-man' or 'man-supporting-God', and that is to imply that Christ is no more than a prophet. The prophets were people on whom God 'rested' for a while, thereby inspiring them, but no one ever called a prophet 'God incarnate'. If we may use another analogy, a prophet is like a person wearing a radio headset tuned in to heaven: what the radio transmits to him is what he says. But no-one would ever suggest that the headset is *united* with the head on which it rests, and once the programme is over the headset can easily be removed. If we apply this principle to Jesus of Nazareth, we simply transform him into a man uniquely inspired by God, a super-prophet or megaprophet, but not the incarnate Logos. And since no prophet ever did or could bring about the redemption of the human race, a Christ in whom the divine and human natures are separated is no use to Christianity.

Where, then, do we go from here? If we must neither 'confuse' nor 'separate' the natures, how are we to understand the incarnation? The answer lies in the paradoxical expression 'unconfused union', a phrase which is intended to imply (1) that a real personal uniting of Godhead and manhood has taken place, but (2) that in this uniting, the characteristics and properties of both natures are preserved entire and intact. Here we have *distinction* of natures, but not separation, and *uniting* of natures, but not confusion. To find an analogy for this conception is, of course, ultimately impossible, and the best I can do is to symbolize the divinity by light-coloured sand and the humanity by dark-coloured sand, and mix them together. The resultant material now *appears* to be grey, but if we look at it very closely we can still see the individual grains of dark and light sand, and we can also see that not one of them has changed colour. Furthermore, for all prac-tical purposes, we cannot now separate the millions of grains back into their constituent colours, even though we can see them and tell them apart. So what we have here is something which *appears* to be confused, but is not, and something in which the two constituents retain their individual characteristics—dark and light—but cannot be separated once they have been joined together. In other words, we have an *unconfused union,* and that, as we shall see, is the only tolerable Christian alternative.

So much then, for the first general point we need to make. It is certainly the most important of the three, and must be kept in mind throughout the whole discussion which follows. The other two are rather simpler: one is geographical and theological, and the other geographical and political. The former involves Alexandria and Antioch; the latter, Alexandria and Constantinople.

As we saw in Chapter Four, at the end of the second century there developed in Alexandria a famous Catechetical School of which the greatest teachers were Clement and Origen. We also observed in the same chapter how too great a dependence on later Platonic thought could lead to an over-emphasis of the spiritual to the detriment of the temporal, or, in the case of Christ, to too great an emphasis on his divinity at the expense of his humanity. Since Alexandrian theology was also Christian Platonist theology, it will not come as a surprise to find that this emphasis on the divine was one of the most characteristic features of the teaching of the school. Apollinaris, whom we met in the last chapter, was Alexandrian in his theology, and we have seen how his over-emphasis on the divinity of Christ led to a denial of his true humanity (he had no human soul), and how his insistence on the completeness of the union of Logos and flesh led to the idea of 'divine flesh', of a sharing of divine and human attributes—or, in other words, confusion of natures.

The other side of the theological coin was represented by Alexandria's rival: the Catechetical School of Antioch. Whereas Alexandria was always more Greek, more hellenistic, in its views, and leaned always to the mystical and allegorical, Antioch was always more down-to-earth and practical. Antiochene theology looked more to Judaea than to Greece. It tended to be more semitic than hellenistic, and the practical common sense so characteristic of semitic thinking may clearly be seen in the Antiochene stress on the literal and historical meaning of Scripture (rather than on the mystical and allegorical), and in its emphasis on the humanity of Jesus of Nazareth, sometimes at the expense of his divinity. The Antiochenes therefore stressed the *distinction* of the natures in Christ: he was man and he was God. The Alexandrians stressed the *union* of the natures: he was 'the God-man'—*theanthrōpos* in Greek—or God incarnate. The Antiochenes emphasized the features of his true humanity: he rejoiced, he wept, he suffered and died. The Alexandrians emphasized the features of his true divinity: he was God from God, light from light, consubstantial and co-eternal, the divine Logos, God made man. But we must remember that we are only speaking of a difference in emphasis here. The Antiochenes no more denied the divinity of Christ than the Alexandrians denied his humanity. Of course not. But there *was* a difference in approach, and there is no doubt that if we push Antiochene thought to its extreme, the stress on distinction of natures can easily lead to their separation; and if we push Alexandrian thought to its extreme, the stress on the unity of the natures can easily lead to their confusion.

Our third and final point is more political. We noted in Chapter Five that at the Council of Nicaea certain decrees or canons were promulgated which ranked the great metropolitan sees—i.e., the main administrative divisions of the Christian world of the time—in order of precedence. The first in order was Rome (no-one disputed that, or the tradition that the Christian community there had been founded by Saint Peter himself), the second was Alexandria, the third was Antioch in Syria, and the fourth was Caesarea in Palestine (which included Jerusalem). But the Council of Nicaea was held in 325, five years before Constantine officially inaugurated Constantinople as his new imperial capital, and later councils had to decide what to do about the new imperial city. The Second Ecumenical Council, after all, was held in Constantinople in 381. The result was never really in doubt. To the great displeasure of Alexandria, which had hitherto been the most important diocese in the east, Constantinople pushed its way in between Alexandria and Rome, called itself the 'New Rome', relegated Alexandria to third place in diocesan order, and, at the Council of Constantinople in 381, was given 'honorary precedence' over all Churches save Rome itself. Alexandria, we might add, was not the only see to be disturbed. Rome eyed the rise of Constantinople with considerable alarm, and regarded it as a young and upstart puppy snapping at the heels of an older and wiser dog. It is easy to understand, then, that from the end of the fourth century, there was often rivalry and antagonism between the bishops of Constantinople and Alexandria, and certain patriarchs of Alexandria were not averse to using decidedly devious tactics to secure the embarrassment or the deposition of their rivals in the imperial see.

With these lengthy, but essential, preliminary comments behind us, we may now introduce Nestorius. Born sometime in the later fourth century, he was trained in Antioch (note!), and gained a great reputation as a preacher. When the see of Constantinople became vacant in the year 428, Nestorius was appointed as bishop. Like the owner of a new house, the new bishop was eager to clean in all the corners, and this, in theological terms, meant getting rid of those who held heretical, unorthodox, or dangerous opinions. He therefore supported his chaplain, Anastasius, when the latter proclaimed that the use of the title *Theotokos* for the Virgin Mary smacked of Apollinarianism. We must therefore pause for a moment to inquire into the meaning of this title, and ask why it might imply the heretical—and condemned—views of Apollinaris.

First of all, what does *Theotokos* mean? It is derived from two Greek words, *theos* 'god' and *tokos* 'a bringing forth, a birth', and the two together—*Theotokos*—mean 'one who brings forth God'. It is usually translated 'God-bearer', and is the Greek equivalent of the Latin *Dei Genetrix* or (more loosely) *Mater Dei,* 'Mother of God'. The title had been used of Mary from the third century—perhaps even from the second (it may possibly have been used by Hippolytus)—and by the fifth century was universally accepted in the east and widely used.

Secondly, of what was Apollinaris accused? He was accused of denying the true humanity of Christ, and asserting that because of the fusion of divinity and humanity, the flesh of Christ had become, in certain ways, divine. In other words, he was accused of confusing the natures.

Thirdly, how does the first point lead to the second? Consider: was the eternal Godhead ever an infant two or three months old?

Not in any literal sense. Does God have a mother? Not in any literal sense. Did the second person of the Trinity, the divine Logos, wet his bed and mess his diapers? Not in any literal sense. But if we confuse the natures, we *can* say these things; and conversely, if we say these things, we might be implying confusion of natures. What Anastasius and Nestorius said, therefore, was that *Theotokos* or 'God-bearer' was a dangerous term to use, and Nestorius (a good Antiochene, remember, who consequently emphasized the *distinction* of the Godhead and the manhood) suggested that if it was to be used, it should be used only in combination with *anthrōpotokos,* which means 'human-bearer'. And if 'Mary the God-bearer and human-bearer' should prove too much of a mouthful, then the easiest and neatest way out is surely to avoid both and refer to Mary simply and precisely as *Christotokos,* or 'Christ-bearer'.

Furthermore, said Nestorius, just to be on the safe side, it might also be wiser to avoid the term 'union' when speaking of the Godhead and manhood in Christ. The word might possibly imply some confusion of the natures. It might be better to speak of the 'conjunction' of humanity and divinity, since two things 'conjoined' are less likely to be thought of as 'mixed up' or 'amalgamated' or—God forbid!—'confused'. In summary, then, according to the bishop of Constantinople, (1) *Theotokos* is a dangerous term and best avoided; and (2) 'union' is also a dangerous term, and 'conjunction' is better.

It should be added here that Nestorius was neither unique nor original in his proposals. His ideas and, indeed, his terminology had been anticipated by two earlier Antiochenes: Diodore (d. *c.* 390), bishop of Tarsus, and Theodore (*c.* 350–428), bishop of Mopsuestia (the modern town of Misis in southern Turkey, about twenty miles east of Adana). Diodore was a learned man who wrote a large number of treatises, but whose work survives only in fragments. As an Antiochene he stressed the literal interpretation of Scripture and, as we might expect, he was a determined opponent of Apollinaris, whose defective views on the incomplete humanity of Christ he roundly condemned. Theodore was his pupil, and he, too, had no time for the ideas of Apollinaris. Both, therefore, insisted on the presence of a human rational soul in Christ, but both, as staunch Antiochenes, likewise insisted that the human soul and the divine

Logos must not, under any circumstances, be confused. In Diodore's case it seems that the stress on distinction may indeed have come dangerously close to separation, but it is difficult to be certain of this because of the very fragmentary condition of his once voluminous writings. But in Theodore's case, with more material to work from, we may see an excellent example of a devout and orthodox Antiochene attempting, with all his skill, to unite the natures in Christ without confusing them, and to distinguish between them without bringing about their separation.

The precise details of Theodore's Christology are still not wholly clear (and it is beyond the scope of this brief study to attempt to disentangle them), but what seems certain is that, despite his good intentions, the language and terminology he used to express his ideas were somewhat perilous and were certainly open to misinterpretation. On the other hand, no one seems to have noticed this during his lifetime, and when Theodore died in 428, he died as an esteemed and respected bishop of the orthodox church. But when Nestorius died some twenty-three years later, he died as a heretic, deposed and in exile. Why? For two main reasons: first, because Mopsuestia was not Constantinople, and the bishop of Mopsuestia was not the foremost prelate of the eastern Christian world; and secondly, Theodore did not have for his opponent the formidable Cyril, the brilliant but devious bishop of Alexandria, whom we must now introduce upon the stage.

Cyril (d. 444) was a man of acute intellect but violent passions, and detested heretics, Jews, and Later Platonists. He certainly bears some of the responsibility for the brutal murder of the Neoplatonist philosopher Hypatia, a distinguished and learned woman, who was torn to pieces by a Christian mob in Alexandria in 415. Above all, he detested Nestorius. As bishop of Alexandria, he disliked Nestorius as bishop of Constantinople (that upstart and interfering see); as an Alexandrian theologian he disliked him as an Antiochene; and as Cyril he loathed him personally as Nestorius. He and his party therefore began to spread the rumour—partly, perhaps, from misunderstanding, but also partly from malice—that Nestorius would not refer to Mary as the God-bearer because he did not believe that Jesus was God. For if Mary did not give birth to God, to what did she give

oad, and dissolved the council. At this time, we might add,
is also had problems within his own household. He had
n a weak man, and had the misfortune to be associated
very strong women: his elder sister Pulcheria and his wife
When we learn that his sister strongly supported Cyril and
ongly supported Nestorius, we can only sympathize with
or whose home life, religious life, and political life were
chaos.

point Theodosius placed both Cyril and Nestorius under
t while he decided what to do, but during this period the
le Cyril, by a little persuasion and a great deal of bribery
a was a rich diocese), enticed a considerable number of
people into the anti-Nestorian camp. Nestorius, at this
ed what was happening, seems to have lost heart, and ef-
ve up the struggle. He wanted nothing more to do with
and requested that he be allowed to return to Antioch,
ter the monastery in which he had been trained and to
s in peace. Part of his wish was granted: he was indeed
to go back to his monastery, but only for a few years. In
osius banned his books, and soon afterwards he was ban-
emote oasis in the Libyan desert, and there, in obscurity,
ortly after 451.

is's retirement from the fray still left certain difficulties
primarily the rift between Cyril and John of Antioch.
or was still demanding that something be done, and Cyril,
estorius had left the field, could afford to be more lenient.
was forced to be very lenient indeed, and although both
dispute had no choice but to compromise, it was Cyril
compromise more. In 433 he and John signed the so-
ula of Reunion, which stated, amongst other things, that

y-begotten Son of God, perfectly God and perfectly
, with a rational soul and body. Before the ages begotten from the Father in his divinity, and in these
s, for us and for our salvation, [he was begotten]
ary the Virgin in his humanity. He is consubstantial

birth? The answer is obvious: she gave birth to a man, an ordinary human child just like any one of us, who was then 'adopted' by God or 'taken over' by God or 'inspired' by God, and thereby transformed into Christ. Later theologians would refer to this heretical doctrine as Psilanthropism, a word which derives from the Greek words *psilos* 'mere' and *anthrōpos* 'human being', and which may therefore be translated as 'mere-man-ism'. But 'mere-man-ism' obviously separates the natures and classes Christ with the prophets—they, too, were mere men inspired by God—and it denies one of the basic presuppositions of the Christian faith: namely, that Jesus of Nazareth was God incarnate, and was God incarnate from his conception.

Cyril, therefore, became the champion of the *Theotokos,* the most vociferous defender of the term, maintaining again and again that if you are unsure of the title, you are likewise unsure of the divinity of Christ. Christ was God from his conception, true God and true man, and if Nestorius thinks otherwise (which, we might add, he did not), then he is a heretic and no Christian. Cyril also objected to Nestorius's use of the term 'conjunction'. For Nestorius, it was the safest term to use, since 'union' could so easily imply confusion (Nestorius had a point), and although occasionally he did use the word 'union', he was not especially happy in doing so. Cyril looks at the matter from quite the opposite point of view: 'conjunction' implies *separation* of natures; it is 'union' which is safe! 'Conjoining' implies nothing more than a loose bond, an incidental relationship, and is only to be expected from someone like Nestorius, who, as everyone knew, was an Antiochene heretic who disbelieved in the divinity of Christ. How do you tell orthodox Christians from the other variety? By listening to their language. If they freely and happily use the terms *Theotokos* and 'union', they are orthodox. If they do not, suspect the worst.

Now it is easy—too easy—in this exchange to see Nestorius as the wholly innocent party and Cyril as his evil demon: to see Nestorius as the spotless lamb of Constantinople devoured by the fury of the Alexandrian dragon. Such a view would be unfair and inaccurate, for although the intentions of Nestorius were good, his actions lacked tact, his language was often provocative and incautious, and in his description of the linkage of the Godhead and manhood in

Christ, he used terms with the most unfortunate implications. The conjunction, he said (following Theodore of Mopsuestia, who may have been his teacher), was 'according to *eudokia*', a Greek expression which could be translated as 'by grace, favour, good pleasure, or good will'. And whatever Nestorius (and Theodore) meant by it (and that is not altogether clear), there is no doubt that this is also the way God dwells in or with his prophets and saints. But if Christ is no more than a super-prophet or maxi-saint, Nestorius has separated the natures and denied the possibility of salvation. Nestorius, of course, never intended this, and never, at any time, denied Christ's divinity. On the other hand, his terminology was unquestionably unsound, and Cyril, who, despite his other faults, was a very good theologian, was perfectly correct in castigating it. On the other hand, Nestorius never said that Jesus was a mere man, nor did he refuse to use the title *Theotokos,* and Cyril's presentation of his views was, without doubt, maliciously exaggerated.

Throughout 430, in a series of important letters (the second and third Synodical Epistles) and dogmatic treatises, Cyril worked for the downfall of Nestorius. As a consequence of this, late in that year, Nestorius himself petitioned the emperor Theodosius II (the grandson of Theodosius I and a man as genuinely pious as he was politically incompetent) to summon a council to discuss the question. Theodosius agreed, for he realized the seriousness of the situation and hoped to settle the controversy at this synod. His hopes, however, were doomed to disappointment. From the point of view of conciliar procedure, the Council of Ephesus—the third Ecumenical Council—was a disaster; and whether, at the end of it, it was Nestorius or Cyril who was condemned depended entirely on the party to which you belonged.

Theodosius called the council for early June 431, but many bishops, including Nestorius's chief supporter, John of Antioch, found it impossible to reach Ephesus in time. He and others were delayed by bad weather and unfavourable winds. Cyril immediately took advantage of their absence and (improperly) opened the proceedings on 22 June. By that date there were about two hundred bishops present, most of them passionately antagonistic to Nestorius and/or the see of Constantinople. The imperial representative at the council, a man

named Candidianus, objected to w
wholly irregular procedure, and de
latecomers. Cyril, however, simply ig
the first session of the council. Hard
majority condemned and deposed
defend himself. He was at home, h
(for his own protection), and he ref
all the bishops who were supposed

John of Antioch and a number of
days later, and when they discovered
their own council on 26 June unde
counter-council—again not surpr
condemned and deposed. Both sid
to Theodosius and waited to hear h
going on, the three western represe
rived, even later than John, but they
the pope to side with Cyril.[1] Cyril,
had again turned in his direction, re
Roman delegates in attendance. In
this pro-Cyrilline council rubber-s
taken by Cyril, and in a further se
condemned and deposed John of An
eastern bishops who had supported

The two final sessions of the coun
importance, though in the session
(Canon 7) that henceforth the only
the Creed of Nicaea promulgated in
one was to introduce, write, or comp
see, was to have consequences twent

Meanwhile, Theodosius had cons
flicting parties and had decided, in ty
both of them were correct. In early
both Nestorius and Cyril, rejected a

1. At a Roman synod held in August 430
Nestorius, and had charged Cyril with exe

good and
Theodos
always be
with two
Eudokia.
his wife s
an empe
all alike i

At thi
house ar
indefatig
(Alexand
influenti
stage, rea
fectively
the matt
there to
end his
permitte
435 The
ished to
he died

Nesto
unresolv
The emp
now tha
In fact,
sides in
who ha
called *F*
Christ v

the
hur
was
last
fro

(*homoousios*) with the Father in his divinity and consubstantial (*homoousios*) with us in his humanity; and since there has come to be a union of two natures, we therefore confess one Christ, one Son, one Lord. As a consequence of this idea of unconfused union, we confess the holy Virgin to be *Theotokos,* because God the Word became flesh and became human, and from the moment of conception united to himself the temple [= the body] which he took from her.[2]

We must pay careful heed to the language of this document, for the terms used are loaded terms and cannot be appreciated without an understanding not only of the Nestorian controversy, but also of the Arian and Apollinarian controversies which preceded it: 'with a rational soul and body', 'begotten from the Father, *'homoousios'*, 'union of two natures', 'unconfused union', *'Theotokos'*, 'became flesh and became human', 'from the moment of conception'. Every word here is calculated and deliberate. Not one is insignificant or accidental.

By signing this document, John and Cyril established an uneasy peace which was to last for some fifteen years. But because of the compromises involved (and as we might expect, the hard-liners on both sides had no time for any compromise), it was a peace which was built on sand and was doomed eventually to be overthrown. The great controversy was dormant, but not ended, and, as we shall see in the next chapter, when it flared up again, it flared up with even greater heat than before.

In a chapter such as this, it is easy to lose one's way among the political intrigues and double-dealing, and fail to see what lay at the heart of the christological problem. It is also easy, as we said earlier, to portray Nestorius and Cyril as incarnations of good and evil (or evil and good) respectively, and thereby do both of them a grave injustice. There is no doubt that both were striving for the same theological end: to avoid the unacceptable extremes of confusion of natures

2. Translated from Cyril of Alexandria's letter to John of Antioch (23 April 433); T. H. Bindley, rev'd. F. W. Green, *The Oecumenical Documents of the Faith* (London, 1950 [4th ed.]) 142.

and separation of natures, and to make it incontrovertibly clear that
the only tolerable doctrine was that there is in the one Christ an
unconfused union of true God and true man. The problems lay in
terminology—*Theotokos* v. *Christotokos,* conjunction v. union—and
also, it must be admitted, in Cyril's antagonism and underhand tactics. Yet we must not forget that underneath the unethical schemer
there lay a very sound theologian. His second letter to Nestorius,
which was written in February 430 and which was given conciliar
approval at Ephesus, is a fine piece of work, and both his trinitarian
and christological writings demonstrate the precision and acuity of
his thinking. Nor were his vehement attacks on Nestorius entirely
without foundation. There is certainly no doubt that the latter was
maligned, but there is equally no doubt that some of his ideas—and
particularly his terminology—were indeed dubious. On the other
hand, he did *not* say that Christ was a mere man, and there is a world
of difference between using words which are unwise and making
statements which are wrong. We might say that Cyril's theology was
superior to his morals, whereas Nestorius's morals were superior to
his theology.

This icon depicts Mary the God-bearer with her divine and human Son. The Virgin supports the Christ-child on her left arm and points to him with her right hand. This type of icon is therefore known as *Theotokos Hodegetria*, which means 'The God-bearer showing the way'—the way being Christ, who is the way to salvation. To the left and right of Mary's halo we see (in Greek) her title 'Mother of God', and above the halo of the Christ-child is, again in Greek, I<ĒSOU>S CH<RISTO>S, 'Jesus Christ'. Jesus himself holds in his left hand the scroll of the new dispensation, and bestows a blessing with his right. This is the most common type of icon depicting the Virgin, and—according to an ancient but very dubious tradition—it was a type first painted by Saint Luke the Evangelist.

THEOTOKOS HODEGETRIA

Icon by Eileen McGuckin
Location: The Icon Studio, New York
Photo: Eileen McGuckin

THE COUNCIL OF CHALCEDON

THE UNEASY PEACE of 433 came to an end in 448. By this time
John of Antioch had been dead for seven years and Cyril of Alexandria for four. How Nestorius reacted to the death of the latter we
do not know, but there is no doubt that many (especially those with
Antiochene sympathies) received the news with glee. One writer,
possibly (but not certainly) Theodoret, bishop of Cyrrhus in Syria,
wrote a letter to Domnus, bishop of Antioch, which began 'At long
last the villain has gone'. The good and gentle, he continued, die
all too soon; it's the bad who go on living forever. Indeed, said the
writer, although those who have survived Cyril may be delighted
at his departure, we can't say the same for the dead. They might be

so irritated with his company as to send him back. God forbid! So we need to tell the undertakers to lay a really big heavy stone on his grave to make sure he stays there.[1]

In 448 Nestorius himself was still in exile in the Libyan desert and Theodosius II was still nominally emperor, though he was now being dominated by the immensely influential Grand Chamberlain of the imperial court, the eunuch Chrysaphius. The bishop of Constantinople was Flavian, a well-meaning but weak prelate, and in Rome, the papacy had passed from Sixtus III, who had assisted in achieving the truce of 433, to Leo the Great, that forceful, energetic, and charismatic figure who was so important for the development of papal power in the fifth century.

Chrysaphius's godfather was Eutyches (c. 378–454), the archimandrite—or, in western terms, abbot—of one of the major monasteries in Constantinople. By this time he was probably about seventy, and whether from senility or some other cause, his thinking was fuddled and his theology poor. Leo called him an imprudent, inexperienced, ignorant old man who should have known better. He was wholly anti-Nestorius and wholly pro-Cyril, but in his support of the Cyrilline cause, he went further than ever Cyril did, and fell headlong into the pit that yawns at the outer edge of Alexandrian christology: he confused the natures in Christ. Just how he confused them, and to what extent, is not entirely clear. Eutyches himself may not have known, for as we have said, his theological thinking left much to be desired. He certainly maintained that, although there were two natures before the incarnation, there was only one nature afterwards (which can be dangerous talk), and he certainly envisaged Christ's humanity as being somehow swallowed up or absorbed by the divinity. This, of course, is to deny that Christ was consubstantial with us, and it imperils the Christian doctrine of redemption. In other words, whatever it was that Eutyches was saying, there is no doubt that it was wrong. He *did* confuse the natures, and his views were unquestionably heretical.

---

1. Theodoret of Cyrrhus (?), *Epistola,* 180.

Late in 448 the matter came to a head. Eutyches, his godson Chrysaphius, and Dioscorus, Cyril's successor as bishop of Alexandria (who, like Eutyches, was an extremist in the Cyrilline party and considered Constantinople to be far too big for its boots), determined to put an end to the truce of 433. Eutyches, therefore, who was an important and highly respected figure in Constantinople (despite his theological inadequacies), began openly to condemn those who maintained that after the union of Godhead and manhood in the incarnation, there still remained two natures. Almost immediately he was accused of confusing the natures (which was true), and of resurrecting the heresy of Apollinaris (which was partly true).

The case came before Flavian, bishop of Constantinople, at a synod in November 448. Flavian realized immediately that Eutyches' views were unacceptable, and he had no hesitation in saying so. He and the other bishops at the synod therefore condemned his ideas and deposed him. But Eutyches challenged the accuracy of the minutes (it seems, in fact, that there might indeed have been errors), appealed the sentence, and wrote, defending himself, to a number of important bishops, including his friend Dioscorus of Alexandria (who he knew would support him) and the powerful Leo in Rome (who he hoped would support him). Dioscorus, of course, rallied round straightaway, and with their tremendous influence at court, he, Eutyches, and Chrysaphius persuaded the emperor to review the case at a council to be held at Ephesus in August 449. Leo, meanwhile, had read Eutyches' appeal and had, at first, been sympathetic. But then he received the minutes of the trial, which had been sent to him by Flavian. He realized at once that Eutyches' views could not possibly be countenanced, and that Flavian and his fellow-bishops had been right to depose him. Leo therefore prepared a statement of the case—later given the name the *Tome of Leo*—and sent it off to Flavian, assuming that it would be read at the council in August. The *Tome* was actually compiled by the pope's secretary, Prosper of Aquitaine, but it was issued under Leo's name, and therefore carried his authority. It may well have been revised and edited by him.

The Emperor Theodosius, who had called the council, envisaged it as being ecumenical, and, accordingly, Leo had sent four western delegates (one of whom died *en route*) to represent him and present his case. The council opened on 8 August under the presidency of Dioscorus, but when the western bishops asked that Leo's *Tome* be read out, the wily Dioscorus circumvented their request. It would, of course, be read (said he), but surely, for the moment, the emperor's own letters should take precedence. And despite a number of later attempts by the western representatives, there was always a reason why the *Tome* should not be read just at that particular time, and by the end of the council it had not been read at all. The council, in fact, was dominated by Dioscorus, and there was never the slightest doubt about its outcome. By a mixture of cajolery, threats, and just plain violence, Dioscorus had Eutyches reinstated and Flavian condemned and deposed. Flavian was then led away under guard, imprisoned in Ephesus, and exiled shortly afterwards, but he did not live to reach the place of his exile. After about four days on the road, he died from a mixture of exhaustion and ill treatment.

Back in Rome, Leo was, naturally, incensed. As far as he was concerned, he was the bishop of the foremost see of Christendom and the true successor of Saint Peter. More than that, he saw himself as the very voice of Peter, and if he declared that Eutyches, or anybody else for that matter, was wrong, then that was all there was to it. He referred to the council as a 'den of thieves' (*latrocinium* in Latin) and prepared to do battle. In October 449, he began a letter-writing campaign to the emperor and others demanding that a new council be held in Italy to reconsider the entire matter, but his efforts had no effect. Theodosius could or would do nothing, and, to the delight of Dioscorus and Chrysaphius, stated that he was quite content with the resolutions of the August 449 council.

But the triumph of Chrysaphius and Eutyches was short-lived. In the course of the following year, Chrysaphius was ousted by Pulcheria (Theodosius II's elder sister; we met her in the last chapter), and Theodosius himself fell off his horse, sustained serious injuries, and died on 28 July 450. Things now moved very swiftly. Pulcheria married Marcian, an intelligent soldier who then became the new emperor, Leo allied himself with Pulcheria, Chrysaphius was executed, and Dioscorus trembled in his episcopal shoes. Then, to resolve the chaotic situation and provide a solution to these involved and violent controversies, Marcian summoned a council to meet in October 451. The original intention was to hold the council at Nicaea, but at the emperor's request it was transferred to Chalcedon—on the Bosphorus, just opposite Constantinople—and opened on 8 October 451 in the church of Saint Euphemia the Martyr.

This was the great Council of Chalcedon, the fourth Ecumenical Council, and the largest the Church had hitherto seen. More than five hundred bishops attended, all but five of whom were easterners. There were also some imperial representatives, and since the real powers behind the council were Pulcheria and Leo, the results (despite much discord and many difficulties) were predictable. The decisions of the council of August 449—Leo's 'den of thieves'—were annulled. Dioscorus was deposed and died three years later in exile at Gangra (now Cankiri in Turkey, about sixty miles north-east of Ankara). Flavian, two years dead, was posthumously reinstated. Eutyches was banished—he was still alive in exile in 454, but what happened to him after that is unknown. Nestorius was re-condemned, though it made little difference to him since his life was almost over. And Cyril of Alexandria (seven years in his grave) and Leo of Rome (very much alive) were treated as inspired spokesmen of orthodoxy.

The emperor and his wife—Marcian and Pulcheria—then required the council to draw up a document summarizing the results of its deliberations. This request—demand would be a better term—was not well received by the bishops, and many of them strongly objected to it. The non-Christians of the Empire used to ridicule the Church for what appeared to be its principle of 'different council, different creed', and there was determined opposition to yet another credal statement. But, not unexpectedly, the will of the imperial house prevailed, and a small committee, chaired by Anatolius, patriarch of Constantinople, was instructed to prepare a draft. Eventually, after much discussion and some passionate argument, a revised edition of this draft became the document known as the *Chalcedonian Definition of the Faith,* and we must now examine its contents in some detail.

In essence, the *Chalcedonian Definition* makes five points as follows:

Point 1: It sets out and agrees with the 'Creed of the Three Hundred and Eighteen Holy Fathers'. This is the creed composed at the Council of Nicaea in 325, which we translated and discussed in

Chapter Five. The number 318, as we explained there, is theological, not literal. The re-statement of this creed as the first point in the *Definition* is important, for, as we pointed out in the last chapter, the seventh canon of the Council of Ephesus, issued on 22 July 431, declared that henceforth no-one should introduce, write, or compose any creed other than the Creed of Nicaea. The bishops at Chalcedon were well aware of this, and it was one of the reasons why so many were so loath to prepare a new definition. But even though the pressure from Marcian and Pulcheria made a new definition inevitable, the least the bishops could do was to place the old Creed of Nicaea in the first and most honourable place.

Point 2: 'Because of those who fight against the Holy Spirit', the *Definition* sets out and agrees with the creed of the 'One Hundred and Fifty Holy Fathers who assembled in the imperial city'. 'Those who fight against the Holy Spirit' were the Pneumatomachi or Pneumatomachians, whom we discussed in Chapter Six, and the 'One Hundred and Fifty Holy Fathers who assembled in the imperial city' refers to the second Ecumenical Council, the Council of Constantinople, which met in 381. But if the Creed of Nicaea was to be the *only* creed of the Christian Church, how can we explain or defend the appearance of this second creed? The answer is simple: it was not regarded as a second creed, but as an appendix to the Creed of Nicaea which elaborated and clarified the question of the Holy Spirit. But exactly what this creed is, what it says, and how it is connected with the council of 381, are matters we shall return to a little later.

Point 3: The *Definition* agrees with the 'synodical letters of the blessed Cyril, shepherd of the church of Alexandria' because they refute the follies of Nestorius. When they drafted this third point, the bishops at Chalcedon were probably thinking only of Cyril's second letter to Nestorius (which we mentioned in Chapter Nine), written in February 430, and his letter to John of Antioch, written 23 April 433, which contains the text of the *Formula of Reunion*. But it was not long before Cyril's third letter to Nestorius, which dates from November 430 and represents a much more extreme Cyrilline position, was also understood to be included.

Point 4: The *Definition* agrees with the 'Letter of the leader of the great and older Rome (Constantinople, remember, was the 'New'

Rome), the most blessed and most holy archbishop Leo' because it refutes the perverse ideas of Eutyches. This is the *Tome of Leo* which we mentioned above, in which Leo, in clear and precise Latin, shows just why Eutyches was wrong and demonstrates that Christianity *must* accept a doctrine in which 'the properties of each nature and substance were preserved, and came together into one person . . . Therefore, in the complete and perfect nature of true man there was born true God: complete in what belonged to him, complete in what belonged to us.'[2] In other words, the doctrine of unconfused union, with which we are now so familiar.

Point 5: Finally, after disposing of Nestorianism and Eutychianism, the bishops at Chalcedon set out as clearly and as concisely as possible what they considered to be the true, official, orthodox position of the universal church with regard to the person of Christ. Some of the language was drawn from Cyril's second letter to Nestorius; some was taken from Leo's *Tome* (and, of course, translated into Greek); a little of it derives from statements of bishop Flavian; and a considerable amount was borrowed from the *Formula of Reunion* which we discussed and, in part, translated in the last chapter. What they said was this:

> Therefore, following the holy fathers, we all unanimously teach that we should confess that our Lord Jesus Christ is one and the same Son, the same perfect in his divinity, the same perfect in his humanity, truly God and truly man, with a rational soul and body, consubstantial (*homoousios*) with the Father in his divinity and consubstantial (*homoousios*) with us in his humanity, like us in all things except for sin; before the ages begotten from the Father in his divinity, and in the last days, for us and for our salvation, [begotten] from Mary the Virgin, the *Theotokos,* in his humanity. He is one and the same Christ, Son, Lord, only-begotten, made known in two natures without confusion, without change, without division, without separation. The difference of the

2. Leo I the Great, *Epistola* (28) *dogmatica ad Flavianum,* 3.

natures is in no way removed because of the union, but, rather, the specific property of each of the two natures is preserved, and they come together in one person and one subsistence, not parted or divided into two persons, but one and the same Son and only-begotten God the Word, Lord Jesus Christ.[3]

To western eyes this was an unambiguous and clear-cut statement. It is as precise a description as could be hoped for of the doctrine of unconfused union, and if we read it in context, with the whole document of which it forms the concluding part, it is quite impossible to retain any doubts about the blasphemous unacceptability of Nestorian separation or the iniquitous folly of Eutychian confusion. There is one person of the incarnate Christ, and in that one person are the two united natures of true God and true man. There is no confusion, no change, no division, and no separation. Nothing could be more precise, and, after some initial hesitation, the west accepted the *Chalcedonian Definition* and remained true to it from the time of Leo the Great onwards. We might add that even this initial hesitation was related, not to what was said of Christ, but to what was said of Constantinople. Canon 28 of the council claimed equal privileges for New Rome and Old Rome, and that was something which Leo—Peter *redivivus*—was certainly not going to accept. But apart from the controversy over Canon 28, the west accepted the *Chalcedonian Definition* as the final statement of orthodox christology.

In the east, unfortunately, this was not the case, but before discussing the reasons for this, we must return for a moment to the second point made by the bishops at Chalcedon and say a few words about the creed of the '150 Holy Fathers'. This is the most widely used creed among Christians of all varieties, both eastern and western, and, according to long tradition—see below— it is most often referred to as 'the Nicene Creed.' This appellation, however, is as unfortunate as it is incorrect, since it confuses it with the original 325 Creed of

---

3. Translated from the Greek text in T. H. Bindley, revd. F. W. Green, *The Oecumenical Documents of the Faith* (London, 1950 [4th ed.]) 193.

Nicaea which we examined in Chapter Five. On other occasions it appears as 'the Nicene-Constantinopolitan Creed', or just 'the Constantinopolitan Creed', a title which implies the traditional tale of its origin. According to this tradition, what we have here is the original Creed of Nicaea with additions and elaborations made by the bishops at the Council of Constantinople in 381. These additions and elaborations were intended to refute certain heretical ideas about the Holy Spirit which had arisen since 325, and which obviously could not have been dealt with in the original version. We are referring here to the ideas of the Pneumatomachians, who refused to accept the full divinity of the Spirit, or refused to associate the Spirit with the *ousia* of the Father and Son.

It is now known that this tradition is incorrect, but precisely what did happen is still not wholly clear. The most probable explanation seems to be that the creed originally derived from the Jerusalem church—though this is not certain—and that by 374 it already existed in a form identical or almost identical to that in which it was received at Constantinople in 381. Whether the bishops at Constantinople made revisions to the text—and, if so, how many—is likewise unclear. But one thing is certain: whatever its origin, very little notice was taken of the creed between 381 and 451, and its present fame and wide-spread usage dates from what we might call its 'canonization' by the Council of Chalcedon. Here is a literal translation of this creed:

> We believe in one God, Father, almighty, maker of heaven and earth, and of all things visible and invisible; and in one Lord Jesus Christ, the only-begotten Son of God begotten from the Father before all ages, light from light, true God from true God, begotten not made, consubstantial (*homoousios*) with the Father, through whom all things came into being; who, because of us humans and because of our salvation, came down from the heavens and became incarnate from the Holy Spirit and Mary the Virgin and became human, and was crucified for us under Pontius Pilate, and suffered and was buried, and rose on the third day according

to the Scriptures, and ascended into the heavens, and sits
on the right hand of the Father, and will come again with
glory to judge the living and the dead, of whose kingdom
there will be no end; and [we believe] in the Holy Spirit,
the lord and life-giver, who proceeds from the Father, who
with Father and Son is together worshipped and together
glorified, who spoke through the prophets; in one holy
universal and apostolic church. We confess one baptism to
the remission of sins; we look forward to a resurrection of
the dead and a life of the world to come. Amen.

A careful comparison of this creed with the original Creed of
Nicaea (translated in Chapter Five) reveals a number of minor and
two major differences. The major differences are (1) the whole of
the last paragraph dealing with the Holy Spirit, and (2) the important addition 'of whose kingdom there will be no end'. To understand these additions we must remember that although this creed
was 'canonized' at Chalcedon, it actually dates from the late fourth
century, and the section on the Holy Spirit reflects the efforts of the
Cappadocian Fathers—Basil and the two Gregories—to complete
the work of Athanasius and to persuade people to accept a Trinity
in which all three persons, and not just the Father and the Son, were
consubstantial. But notice the cautious way in which the passage is
phrased: the Holy Spirit is described in biblical terms ('lord' comes
from 2 Cor 3:17, and 'life-giver' from Rom 8:2), and is simply said
to be 'co-worshipped and co-glorified' with Father and Son. This
certainly *implies* the full divinity of the Holy Spirit, but it does not
actually say it, and nowhere in this final paragraph is the Holy Spirit
specifically referred to as 'God', or declared unequivocally to be
homoousios with the other two persons of the Trinity. By 451 this
cautious Basilian language would hardly have been necessary, but the
Chalcedonian Fathers were not prepared to devise a new creed, and
were unwilling to tamper with those already in existence. They preferred to remain true to the tradition they had received (or thought
they had received) from their predecessors, and therefore stated that
the section of the 'Constantinopolitan' Creed which dealt with the
question of the substance/*ousia* of the Holy Spirit simply clarified

the very brief statement with which the original Creed of Nicaea concluded. They stressed, however, that it was clarification, not addition, for there was nothing at all lacking in the original Nicene Creed. It was simply in need of a certain amount of refinement.

The other passage we mentioned earlier—'of whose kingdom there will be no end'—also derives from a fourth-century milieu. At that time a certain Marcellus was bishop of Ancyra (the modern Ankara in Turkey), and despite the fact that he did not die until about 374, his views on the Trinity echoed the ideas of an earlier century. In some ways he was similar to Hippolytus and Tertullian, who were more or less on the right side of orthodoxy, and in some ways he was similar to Praxeas, who certainly was not. According to Marcellus, in the beginning there was simply a Divine Oneness, One Alone, and only for the purposes of creation and redemption did this Divine Oneness become a Divine Threeness. Only for creation and redemption were Christ the Logos and the Holy Spirit put forth as separate entities, and when the work of redemption has finally been completed, they will be reabsorbed back into the one Source of All Things. At that time, God will once again be 'all in all' (1 Cor 15:28). Marcellus could turn to Saint Paul to support his case—'then comes the end, when he [Christ] delivers the kingdom to the God and Father' (1 Cor 15:24)—but this was emphatically not the view of the Christian Church. As we have seen earlier, Christianity maintains that God was *always* three and one, and to assert that there was once a time and will again be a time when he will be One Alone is to imply that Christianity differs from Judaism only for a limited period. The 'Constantinopolitan' Creed therefore corrects the unacceptable views of Marcellus: since there is no end to Christ, neither is there any end to his kingdom.

Only one final point remains to be considered. The original version of the 'Constantinopolitan' Creed states quite clearly that the Holy Spirit 'proceeds from the Father'. Notice that it does not say that the Spirit proceeds 'from the Father *and the Son*'. Whereas the eastern churches maintained, and still maintain, the original wording, the western churches have generally amended the text to include the additional words: three of them—'and the Son'—if we are thinking in English; only one—*filioque*—if we are thinking in Latin.

Why? The answer is simple: because of Augustine of Hippo. As we saw at the end of Chapter Seven, Augustine's great contribution to the doctrine of the Holy Spirit was to replace the idea of Single Procession ('from the Father *through* the Son') with that of Double Procession ('from the Father *and* the Son'), and this idea rapidly became the accepted teaching of the western church. For more than a century, Latin Christians retained the original wording of the creed, but then, in the late sixth century, we find the additional 'and the Son/*filioque*' appearing first of all in Spain (at the third Council of Toledo to be precise, held in 589), and then, slowly but insidiously, it spread to the Carolingian Empire, and then throughout the whole of Europe until, by the eleventh century, it was accepted at Rome and universally in the Latin west. The east always objected to it, maintaining that creeds promulgated by ecumenical councils cannot be changed except by the authority of ecumenical councils, and that the doctrine was theologically suspect because it destroyed the balance of the Trinity and denied the personhood of the Spirit. But the details of the eastern objections to this brief addition, and the story of how it came to play a major role in the eventual schism of the eastern and western churches in 1054, are matters to be dealt with in a separate study.[4]

For the west, then, the Council of Chalcedon effectively ended the christological dispute. The *Chalcedonian Definition* did not explain *how* the divinity and humanity were united in the one person of Jesus of Nazareth (something wholly inexplicable), but it did state that they *were* united, and that they were united without confusion, change, division, or separation. The situation in the east, however, was more complex and much more violent, and we must now spend a little time in discussing the problems which arose.

4. See D. N. Bell, *Many Mansions. An Introduction to the Development and Diversity of Medieval Theology West and East* (Kalamazoo/Spencer, 1996) Chapter Ten.

Saint maximos

The Confessor

GOD IS THE TRUE GOAL OF ALL LONGING ALL DESIRE AND ALL LOVE

Maximus (Maximos in Greek) (*c.* 580–662) came from an old aristocratic family and was secretary to the emperor Heraclius before becoming a monk in about 614. He was wholly opposed to Monotheletism—the doctrine that in Christ there are two natures but a single will—and was instrumental in having it condemned as heretical at a number of church councils. The emperor Constans II, who had succeeded Heraclius and who supported Monotheletism, was infuriated at this, and had Maximus arrested. Since he remained obdurate after harsh questioning, his tongue was torn out and his right hand cut off. He was then sent into exile, and died shortly afterwards on 13 August 662.

MAXIMUS THE CONFESSOR

Icon by Eileen McGuckin
Location: The Icon Studio, New York
Photo: Eileen McGuckin

XI

CHRIST AFTER CHALCEDON

HAD THE COUNCIL OF CHALCEDON been conducted in Latin and its *Definition* written in Latin for a Latin-speaking world, the bigotry, bitterness, and murder which ravaged the eastern church after the council might have been reduced. It would not have been reduced to nothing, for theological difficulties were often masks for political and nationalistic problems, but it might certainly have been ameliorated. If we say, in Latin as in English, that Christ was one person (*persona*) in whom were united two natures (*naturae*) or substances (*substantiae*), then the statement is unambiguous. 'Substance' does not and cannot mean 'person' in Latin, and we cannot therefore be saying either that Christ was one nature or that he was two persons. In Greek, unfortunately, this was not the case. The Greek word used in the *Chalcedonian Definition* for 'nature' was *physis*. We see it in the English word 'physics', the study of the natural properties of matter, and 'physiology', the study of the processes of natural life. Unfortunately, *physis* could mean not only 'nature' (which was what the bishops at Chalcedon intended it to mean); it could also mean 'individual creature' or 'independent entity' or 'person'. For those who understood the term in this second way, therefore, the statement in the *Chalcedonian Definition* that Christ was 'made known in two natures' (*physeis:* the Greek plural of the word) was out-and-out heresy. According to them, the *Definition* was maintaining that in Christ there were two persons, two separate entities, and to say that was to separate the natures and to resurrect, in all its wickedness, the supposed heresy of Nestorius. If this were indeed the case, the *Chalcedonian Definition* was stating formally, and asking the rest of the Church to accept, that Christ was no more than an inspired man.

Those who understood nature (*physis*) as *person,* therefore, correctly maintained that Christ was not two *physeis,* but one *physis,* and they could defend their view by citing Cyril of Alexandria who, it will be remembered, was treated in the *Chalcedonian Definition* as an infallible voice of orthodox doctrine. Did not Cyril say that in Christ there was '*one* nature (*physis*) of the Word of God enfleshed'? Indeed he did, and by 'nature' he meant the one single, independent person of Jesus of Nazareth. But the extent to which the issue had become confused is apparent when we consider the origin of Cyril's famous phrase. Cyril himself believed it derived from the great Athanasius, but if you turn back to Chapter Eight in this book, you will find that it actually comes, unfortunately, from the heretic and blasphemer Apollinaris.

The situation has clearly become ridiculous. For Apollinaris, 'nature' is 'nature', but for Cyril, quoting Apollinaris (without realizing it), 'nature' is 'person'. For those who supported Chalcedon, 'nature' is 'nature', and for Pope Leo and the west, it is '*natura*' and was never anything else. But for those who opposed Chalcedon and thought they were supporting Cyril, 'nature' is 'person'. Little wonder there was confusion!

Added to this, there were still plenty of people around who had supported Eutyches and still supported him despite the decisions at

Chalcedon, and there still remained a considerable number of Nestorians who still thought Nestorius had been unjustly condemned. The Eutychians, therefore, absolutely refused to acknowledge two natures in Christ, and the Nestorians absolutely refused to acknowledge one. Nor was the conflict limited simply to verbal warfare. Consider the case of Proterius. After Eutyches' friend Dioscorus had been deposed and banished by the Council of Chalcedon in 451, Proterius was appointed in his place as bishop of Alexandria. As a Chalcedonian appointment he naturally supported the *Chalcedonian Definition,* but when he returned to Alexandria he found his Christian flock totally opposed both to it and to him. Alexandria was passionately Cyrilline, and if Cyril had said 'one nature', then 'one nature' it was. So great was the antagonism that Proterius found that he could maintain his position only with military support, but in 457, when the Alexandrians rioted following the death of the emperor Marcian, even this proved worthless. He was set upon by a mob, beaten to death, and his body burned in the local stadium.

In the east, therefore, far from settling the christological problem, Chalcedon had generated further division. On the one hand were the Chalcedonians, those who supported the council and agreed with its *Definition,* and who, like Leo and the West (where *physis* = *natura*), were perfectly happy to acknowledge Christ in two natures. On the other hand was that important group, located primarily in Egypt and Syria (where *physis* = person), who refused to do so, and, following Cyril, would speak only of one nature after the incarnation. This latter group therefore became known as the Monophysites or 'One-nature-ites' and the Chalcedonians, in distinction, as the Dyophysites or 'Two-nature-ites'. But as we said earlier, the terminological differences only concealed much greater nationalistic and political antagonisms. To the Egyptians and Syrians, the Council of Chalcedon appeared as an attempt to impose a foreign—i.e., Greek-Constantinopolitan—imperial domination, for it must be remembered that at this time both the Egyptians and the Syrians had native cultures quite distinct from that of the rest of the Graeco-Roman world. Much of the populace did not even speak Greek—the Syrians spoke Syriac and the Egyptians spoke Coptic (the last stage of Ancient Egyptian)—and in any case, Alexandria and Constantinople had existed for decades in a state of mutual hostility.

'Chalcedonian' and 'Monophysite' thus became nationalistic and political slogans, and, in all probability, there were comparatively few who really understood—or who were much interested in understanding—the subtle theological arguments which lay behind the terminology. To suggest that the conflict could have been resolved theologically would be like saying that the present situation in the Middle East could be remedied simply by persuading Arabs and Jews to admit that the God of Muhammad and the God of Moses are, in fact, precisely the same deity.

Nevertheless, the attempt was made, and since it established a precarious peace for about forty years, it deserves some consideration. In 482, twenty-five years after Marcian had died and Proterius had been lynched, the emperor was Zeno and the patriarch of Constantinople was Acacius, an acute and intelligent man. The patriarch, with the support and sponsorship of the emperor, drew up a compromise proposal called the *Henoticon,* a Greek word which means 'The Unifier' or 'The Uniter'. In this document we find, first, an acceptance of both the Creed of Nicaea and the so-called 'Constantinopolitan Creed', and, secondly, a condemnation of both Nestorius and Eutyches. So far all is in accordance with the *Chalcedonian Definition.* But then, to conciliate the Cyrilline Monophysites, we have, thirdly, an acceptance of Cyril's Twelve Anathemas, which were a series of short anti-Nestorian definitions which were appended to his third Synodical Letter and which represent an extreme form of his teaching; and, fourthly, to conciliate everybody, we have the statement that Christ is consubstantial with the Father in his divinity and with us in our humanity (which was stated in the *Chalcedonian Definition*), that he was incarnate from the Holy Spirit and the Virgin Mary Theotokos (which was also stated in the *Chalcedonian Definition*), and that he is 'one, not two'. Precisely how he is 'one, not two' is not defined, and people could fill in the blanks for themselves. To an Alexandrian Monophysite, he is one (nature); to a Chalcedonian Dyophysite, he is one (person). No-one could deny that Christ was one something, and that was precisely Acacius's point. Fifthly and finally, the *Henoticon* anathematized anyone who held an opinion different from this, 'whether put forward at Chalcedon or at any other council'. But this last statement, alas, did not place the Council of Chalcedon in any good light. It implied, in fact, that its decisions might possibly have been wrong, which had always been the view of the Monophysites.

In the east, this compromise document produced general, if not universal, agreement, and from 482 to about 520 it was accepted as the standard of orthodoxy. But in the west the reaction was very different. Rome objected to the *Henoticon* partly because it conceded that the bishops at Chalcedon might have been misguided (and Rome had accepted the *Chalcedonian Definition* almost from the start), and partly because bishop Acacius had promulgated the *Henoticon* without consulting the pope. Added to this was the further complication that Rome, rather than supporting the bishop who was then occupying the see of Alexandria, Peter Mongus (his name means Peter the Stammerer), was putting all its considerable weight behind a rival claimant, one John Talaia. The consequences were inevitable: Pope Felix III, a stubborn and authoritarian pontiff with a violent temper, was predictably incensed, and in his fury he excommunicated the patriarch of Constantinople in July 484. The sentence of excommunication was sent to the imperial city by special messenger, and eventually pinned to Acacius's vestments by some over-enthusiastic monks while he was in church celebrating the Divine Liturgy. Acacius' response was simply to remove the name of the pope from the diptychs. Why, and so what? Because the diptychs were lists of Christians, living and dead, for whom special prayers were offered at the Eucharist (the term *diptych* refers to the two-leaved folder which contained the lists), and to exclude a particular name from the lists was to imply that the person concerned was not orthodox. It also implied, by extension, that he had been excommunicated. This action marked the beginning of the so-called Acacian Schism, the first schism between the eastern and western churches, which lasted from 484 to the accession to the throne of the emperor Justin I in 518.

Even in the east, however, the *Henoticon* failed to achieve a lasting peace. It is all very well to say 'one, not two', but there comes a time when the problem really cannot be avoided any longer and you feel the need to take the nearest bishop by the throat and ask 'one WHAT?' So despite the appearance in the east of a number of brilliant and sometimes conciliatory theologians during the forty years or so when the *Henoticon* was accepted, the situation gradually deteriorated, and by about 515 the two sides were once again in active opposition.

Other attempts at reconciliation during the sixth century were even less successful than the *Henoticon*. In fact, they were not successful at all. But in the following century, a further effort was made which did seem, at first, to be more effective, but which led to the curious situation wherein a christological doctrine which was patently heretical was approved by the emperor and many of his bishops as the official teaching of Church and state.

As was so often the case, the circumstances which led to this situation were political rather than theological. The eastern emperor, Heraclius, was deeply concerned about increasing attacks on the empire by the Persians and, shortly afterwards, the Arabs, and it would obviously be much to his advantage to reconcile the internal divisions within his realm and face the external aggressors with a united people. He therefore consulted with the Monophysite leaders in 624, and they came up with the suggestion that although it might be admitted that in Christ there were indeed two natures, there was only one 'energy' or 'operation' or 'activity'. The Greek word *energeia* can mean all three things. By this term they meant that it was one and the same Son who was the subject of every activity or operation, and that we must never separate the natures by suggesting that one particular activity pertained to the human son of Mary while another pertained only to the divine Son of God. No longer, therefore, do we speak of 'two natures before the incarnation and one nature after it', or 'two natures in one person'. We now say 'two natures, but one mode of activity'.

Heraclius sent the proposal off to the patriarch of Constantinople, Sergius, who gladly accepted it (he thought he had found a similar idea in the writings of Cyril of Alexandria). And once it had been promulgated, the results, in part, were just what Heraclius had hoped: the Monophysites liked it and flocked back into the orthodox fold. Unfortunately, the hard-line Chalcedonians utterly rejected it, and as a consequence of this rejection, Sergius decided to write to the pope (a good Chalcedonian, as were they all) and seek his opinion.

The pope at the time was Honorius I, an able manager and excellent administrator, but between repairing the Roman aqueducts and managing the papal finances he seems to have had little time to spare for the intricacies of theology. His reply to Sergius, therefore, was both hasty and unfortunate, for not only did he give his approval to the new idea, but went on to say that since it was God the Logos who operated or acted through both natures, this was effectively the equivalent of saying that in Christ there was only one will.

This was more than Heraclius and Sergius had ever hoped for. They seized on the phrase 'one will' with cries of delight, and in 638 Heraclius issued the *Ekthesis* ('The Edict' or 'The Explanation') which stated the official imperial view of the matter: there shall in future be no more mention of 'energies' or 'operations' or 'activities', whether one or two, and all Christians shall confess (whether they like it or not) that there are in Christ two natures united in a single will. Because the Greek word for one is *monos* and the word for will is *thelēma,* this doctrine came to be known as Monotheletism (or Monothelitism: both spellings are used), 'One-will-ism'.

That this doctrine is wrong is not in doubt. From a Christian standpoint, Monotheletism cannot be reconciled with the Christian tradition. To maintain that there is but one will in Christ is, effectively, to deny the real existence and activity of Christ's human will; and to deny a human will in Christ is, in essence, to resurrect the old heresy of Apollinaris which had been condemned two and a half centuries earlier at the second Ecumenical Council. How, then, could Honorius have been so foolish as to suggest it?

Honorius' problem was not foolishness, but haste. He failed to take the care he needed, and there is no doubt that he did *not* mean 'one will' in the sense in which the term appears in the *Ekthesis.* What he meant was that whereas there are *two* wills in Christ—divine and human— there could never be any real conflict between them, for if any conflict did arise, the divine will would ultimately prevail. The bishops at Constantinople in 381 would have agreed. Furthermore, if you have two wills acting in complete harmony and unison, is this really distinguishable from one single will? No, thought Honorius, it is not—and we cannot deny that he has a point. So what he was really saying, but saying very badly, was that although *psychologically* there are two wills in Christ, *functionally* they act in agreement as one.

Honorius died in October 638, just before the *Ekthesis* was issued, but his successors saw immediately that Monotheletism was theologically unsound and, to the great annoyance of the eastern emperor (who saw it as politically essential), had no hesitation in condemning it. This opposition came to a head with the Lateran Council of 649 and the astonishing events surrounding the life and death of Pope Martin I.

By this time Emperor Heraclius was dead and had been succeeded by Constans II. The new emperor, realizing that the *Ekthesis* was causing major problems, withdrew it, and in 647 or 648 substituted for it another edict called the *Typos* ('The Model' or 'The Plan'). But in essence, all that this later document said was that in future no one should speak either of one will or two wills, and that the matter was not a subject for further discussion. Henceforth, the teaching of the Church would be restricted to the definitions of the first five Ecumenical Councils. The fifth, which we do not need to deal with here, had been held in Constantinople in 553. This, of course, was absurd, for human beings have never, at any time, been able to keep their mouths shut, and the surest way of persuading anyone to do anything is to forbid them to do it. Pope Martin, a most courageous man, took the bull by the horns, anathematized Monotheletism, and at the same time condemned outright the imperial *Typos*.

Constans, naturally, was infuriated and immediately ordered the pope to be arrested and brought to Constantinople. He sent one of his chamberlains to do the job, and, in an almost unbelievable series of events, the chamberlain tracked down the pope to the Lateran basilica (where he was ill in bed), deposed him, arrested him, smuggled him out of Rome, imprisoned him for a year on the island of Naxos, and eventually brought him to the imperial capital late in 653. There he was tried, found guilty, flogged, and condemned to death (he already had dysentery and severe gout), but at the request of the patriarch of Constantinople, the death sentence was commuted to banishment. Not that it made much difference to Martin. He was kept in prison for a further three months in revolting conditions, and then taken to the Crimea where, on 16 September 655, he died from starvation, the climate, and just plain brutality. He was the last of the martyr-popes.

Monotheletism lingered on for a further twenty-five years. The west, as we have seen, never accepted it, and eastern theologians, too, were well aware of its dangers. Its most formidable opponent was Maximus—usually called Maximus the Confessor—a learned, ascetic, and holy man who, after holding the post of Imperial Secretary under Heraclius, entered the monastic life in about 614. Maximus, like Martin, realized the inadequacy of Monotheletism, and realized too that the Chalcedonians and the Monophysites were both, at heart, trying to say the same thing: that in Jesus of Nazareth we see an unconfused union of divinity and humanity in one incarnate Lord. But his efforts to make these matters clear earned him imperial disapproval, and Maximus, like Martin, was arrested. Because his tongue, despite imperial orders, had continued to speak of two wills, Constans had it torn out; and because his right hand had refused to sign certain compromising documents, Constans had it cut off. Maximus, too, was exiled, and again like Martin, died soon afterwards, on 13 August 662.

The work of Maximus, Martin, and their colleagues found its fulfilment at the Council of Constantinople in 680 (the sixth Ecumenical Council, held after the death of Constans), which stated unequivocally (1) that in Christ there are two natures; (2) that as a consequence of this there are two wills and two activities; but (3) that there is nevertheless a complete harmony between the divine and human wills, and likewise between the divine and human activities. With the decrees of this council, Monotheletism ceased to be a problem. It had existed for more than fifty years when it should never, really, have come into being; but since it was primarily a political rather than a theological heresy, the theological arguments were often secondary to the political realities.

Monophysitism, on the other hand, never came to an end at all. None of the attempts at reconciliation ever succeeded in achieving any permanent resolution, and although the major part of the Christian world accepted the Chalcedonian statement, from the sixth century until the present, four great Churches have refused to do so: the Armenian, Coptic, Ethiopian, and Syrian Orthodox Churches.

They are still, in terminology, Monophysite, though the designation is now hardly ever used ('Non-Chalcedonian' is the usual term) and most of their theologians recognize that there is no essential difference between the Monophysite and Dyophysite understandings of the person of Christ. At a meeting in 1964, representatives of both streams of Orthodoxy stated officially that they acknowledge in each other the one Orthodox faith, that they find themselves in total agreement on the essential christological dogmas, and that they recognize that the same truth is being expressed in different terminologies. Further meetings with similar irenic consequences have taken place since 1964, but this is obviously not the place to discuss them. From the murder of Proterius to the martyrdom of Martin this, regrettably, was not the case; but whenever theology is transformed into politics, morality and truth take second place to political necessity, and when reason gives way to the rule of the mob, then all of us are doomed.

In this twelfth-century Byzantine mosaic from Sicily, we see a well-muscled Adam and Eve covering their genitals with fig leaves. Having eaten of the Tree of Knowledge (one of the two stylized trees here depicted), they now know that they are naked. At the bottom of the mosaic is the serpent-tempter, and on the left is God, not at all pleased. What he is saying (Gen 3:9–11) appears in Latin at the top of the mosaic.

GOD REPRIMANDING ADAM AND EVE AFTER THE FALL

Location: Duomo (the Cathedral), Monreale, Sicily, Italy
Photo: Scala/Art Resource, New York

XII

A QUESTION OF GRACE

WE HAVE NOW AGREED that Christ the Logos is truly God and consubstantial with the Father and the Holy Spirit. We have also agreed that this divine Word became incarnate in the one unconfused person of Jesus of Nazareth, who was perfect God and perfect man. We have also noted, in both the Creed of Nicaea and the so-called 'Constantinopolitan Creed' that the reason for this incarnation was 'because of us humans and because of our salvation'. How, then, does salvation work? In what way are we to be saved? According to the writer of the letter to the Ephesians, the answer is simple and straightforward: 'You have been saved by grace' (Eph 2:6). But what is grace, how does it work, and how are we to reconcile it with the

155

idea of free-will? Is grace essential, or merely useful? Does everyone need it, or only some? And if I work really hard, live a life of the utmost piety, keep all the commandments, exhibit true charity, and feed all the stray cats in the neighbourhood, can I be saved without it? To answer these questions we must visit the Garden of Eden and see what happened at the Fall.

Both east and west were agreed, first of all, that in Eden Adam and Eve were in a state of blessedness, perfection, and complete happiness. They were immortal, they could talk freely with God, and all their wants, both of body and soul, were fully satisfied. The view of the easterners was somewhat more metaphysical than that of the westerners (Gregory of Nazianzus, for example, visualized the Garden of Eden as the world of the Platonic Ideas), but both were agreed on the essential points.

All Christians, eastern and western, also agreed that Adam and Eve fell. They ate the forbidden fruit and thereby incurred mortality, the potentiality for corruption and disease, and sin. Again, the west laid greater stress than did the east on this last point, but again, both were agreed on the essentials.

Thirdly, all agreed that the consequences of this first sin were not restricted to Adam and Eve, but were in some way passed down to their descendants, namely, us. The process by which this transmission occurred was not quite clear, but that it did occur was not in doubt. One theory held that the soul of a child was generated in some mysterious way from the souls of its parents, much as its body was formed from their bodies; and since the souls of Adam and Eve were tainted before they produced offspring (Cain and Abel were conceived after the expulsion from Eden), the souls they generated were also naturally tainted, and these tainted souls produced, in turn, further tainted souls, all the way down to us. This theory is referred to as *Traducianism*. The Latin verb *traduco* means 'to bring over', and the soul of the infant is 'brought over' from the souls of its parents. If we accept this view, then sin is transmitted like a congenital disease. But although Traducianism makes the transmission of sin easy to understand, the theory was to be condemned by the Church (first of all by Pope Anastasius II in 498), partly because it is difficult to reconcile with the spiritual nature of the soul, and partly because, by suggesting that the souls of children might in some way be produced or generated by the souls of their parents, it imperils the idea of God as the only creator. Instead, the Church approved *Creationism,* the doctrine that each soul is created anew by God at the moment individual existence begins (that there were conflicting opinions as to when this occurred is not significant here), and although this view accounts splendidly for the spirituality of the soul, it makes it much more difficult to explain just how a brand-new creation, straight from the hands of God, could possibly be corrupted by someone else's sin. Yet corrupted it was—of that the theologians were not in doubt—and the only way they could explain it was by proposing a 'spiritual' or 'mystical' unity of later humanity with its first parents. Again, there was a difference of emphasis: the west laid greater stress on this mystical unity than did the east, but neither denied its reality. As a consequence of this inherited taint, our natural inclination is to sin, and we need only glance around the world in which we live to see this inclination in action.

The eastern fathers never denied the existence of free-will and never denied the ability of fallen human beings to do good, even though doing it was difficult. On the other hand, they were also agreed that of one's own power one could never do enough good to achieve salvation. For this we need grace, the supernatural assistance of God. But because we can do *some* good, it is incumbent upon us to do it, and thereby 'deserve' or 'earn' or 'merit' God's further help. By God's grace we were given free-will in the beginning, and by his grace we may use that free-will to do good, and thus become deserving of grace in yet greater abundance. It is like the parable of the prodigal son. The young man who had spent all his money had to make the first move. He had to get up and leave the pigs, and then, while he was still a long way off, his father saw him and came running to meet him. That, for the east, was (and is) how grace operates.

This was also the view of the western fathers up to the time of Augustine. They laid greater stress than did the east on the difficulty of making the first move, but they were, on the whole, convinced that if you do not stir yourself, then you will get nowhere. Neither east nor west believed that the father of the prodigal son was going to send a limousine to collect him, and neither east nor west believed that he would eventually be saved simply by sitting down with the pigs and waiting for something nice to happen.

At this stage, in the early fifth century, Augustine of Hippo came into conflict with Pelagius, and everything changed. Pelagius was British, though in which part of Britain he was born is unknown. He may have been a monk, but was more probably a lay ascetic, and he moved to Rome in about 400. Once there, he acquired a reputation—apparently justified—for his piety, austerity, asceticism, and learning. As a creationist, he could not accept that human beings were so corrupted at birth that they could not help sinning, and he disagreed profoundly with the principle underlying Augustine's prayer to God for control over his sexual urges: 'Give what you command and command what you will.'[1] In Pelagius's view, what Augustine was saying was 'Tell me what to do and then do it for me'. This, surely, is to put the entire burden on God, and as far as the ascetic Pelagius was concerned, it was a denial of free-will and human responsibility—and, as such, an insult to the Creator. If I am not responsible for my vices or virtues, then no just God—if he be truly just—can either blame or praise me. I cannot be criticized for arriving late for an appointment if the taxi in which I am travelling runs out of fuel.

Pelagius, then, as a creationist, takes creationism to its logical conclusion: the soul of an infant is *not* tainted by the sin of Adam and Eve, and every infant has complete freedom of choice to do good or evil. So what about infant baptism? If infants are utterly sinless, newly created from the hand of God, what need is there to wash off non-existent sin? Pelagius's answer is simple: baptism does a lot more than wash off sin. It may indeed be essential for cleansing an adult in adult baptism, but apart from that, it also initiates persons into the Church, which is the Body of Christ, and it bestows upon them the possibility of eternal bliss in the Kingdom of Heaven. How do we know this? Because Saint John says so: 'unless we are born anew of water and the Spirit, we cannot enter the Kingdom of God' (Jn 3:3, 5). It follows, then, that if a newborn baby is to enjoy eternal

---

1. Augustine of Hippo, *Confessions,* X.29.40.

felicity in heaven, that baby must be baptized. For Pelagius, the rite
of baptism looks more to the future than to the past.

But the fact remains that many babies die before baptism. What
happens to them? Augustine had no doubts on the matter, and though
we might doubt his compassion, we cannot refute his logic. Babies,
he says, are born with original sin (we shall see how this is so a little
later). Thus, if that sin is not washed off in baptism, they also die in
original sin. And since sinners go to hell, so do unbaptized babies. It is
true that because their sins are Adam's sins and not their own, they will
suffer 'the lightest possible condemnation',[2] but suffer they will.

To Pelagius and his followers, this was an abominable doctrine.
How can a merciful God condemn infants to suffer for things they
did not do? If unbaptized babies cannot enter the Kingdom of God
(and Pelagius is not going to argue with Saint John), then they will
certainly enter some other place or state of being in which they
will enjoy the utmost natural happiness, even if they are precluded
from the supernatural happiness of the Beatific Vision. Later, in the
Middle Ages, this idea would be codified as the doctrine of limbo or,
more accurately, *limbus infantium,* the limbo of [unbaptized] infants.
As a solution to the problem of the death of unbaptized babies, it
may not be perfect, but it is certainly a more merciful view than
that of Augustine.

So if, according to Pelagius, we are not the recipients of original
sin, does that mean that the Fall had no effect at all? On the contrary.
It had a very profound effect indeed. It set us a bad example, and it
is an example which we tend to follow.

Now it is easy to underestimate Pelagius's teaching on this point.
It is all very well to say that the Fall 'set us a bad example', but why
should we imitate it? If we have complete freedom of will, why not just
say No? The reason becomes clear once we remember that we human
beings are socialized from our birth onwards. How children behave,
and, to a large extent, how they think, is conditioned by the family or
society in which they are brought up, and if they are brought up in a
society in which it is acceptable behaviour to spit on the floor or pick

2. Augustine of Hippo, *Contra Julianum,* 5.44.

one's nose in public, then that is what they will do. It follows, then, that since Adam's children were brought up in a family which had begun to sin, they, too, sinned. And so also did their children and their children's children; and that is why we, too, have just the same problem. We are 'socialized' into sin, 'conditioned' to sin, yet not doomed to sin or forced to sin by any congenital taint or spiritual deformity.

So is there any need for grace, or can we stop this incessant and imitative sinning of our own free will? Pelagius maintains clearly that there is a need for grace (he is often misunderstood on this point), and that grace operates in a number of ways. First of all, there is the grace of free will itself by which we can choose freely between righteousness and wickedness. Secondly, there is the grace of revelation in the Scriptures, both Old and New, by which the paths of good and evil are laid out before us. And thirdly, there is the grace of forgiveness of sins, which operates especially in repentance and penance, and which comes into play when, like all people, we err and stray and fall short of the glory of God. Pelagius, as we have said, insists on the need for all three forms of grace. But why? If sin is simply a habit, why not give it up tomorrow? To appreciate why not, consider yourself. Find a good, solid, ingrained habit (biting your nails, smoking, fiddling with your earrings, saying 'you know?' or 'right?' after every sentence: there will be no difficulty in discovering an example), and stop it. Now. Immediately. And never do it again. *Then* you will see the immense difficulty of the task, and realize that we are as addicted to sin as a heroin addict is to heroin. In theory, we *can* give it up; in practice, most of us need professional help, and in the case of sin, that professional help is the grace of God.

How, then, does grace work for Pelagius? Perhaps the best way to understand it is by using the analogy of a coach and competitors at an athletics event. First of all, the competitors enter the arena with a perfectly free choice of whether and when to run, kick, punch, or jump. Secondly, as the coach, I can stand on the sidelines, shout encouraging comments, and tell the competitors what to do and when to do it. And thirdly, if my team makes a mistake or fails to take my advice, I can tell them that it doesn't really matter, that their sins are forgiven them, that in future they should listen to their coach, but that they don't have to leave the area immediately and throw themselves off the nearest cliff or hang themselves from the nearest tree. But at no time can I enter the ring or the field and add my strength and skill to theirs, and I certainly cannot rush in, open their mouths wide, climb down inside them, and compete for them.

For Pelagius, we are all competitors (competitors with ingrained bad habits) and Christ is the coach. Without his example, instruction, and continual encouragement we, by ourselves, may not be able to triumph, and his presence is therefore essential to us to tell us and show us what to do and how and when to do it. The imitation of Christ lies at the very heart of Pelagius's teaching. But this is as far as he goes. His concept of grace is essentially a concept of 'encouraging' or 'exhortatory' grace, whereas the great majority of the other Christian theologians of his time preferred to think in terms of 'assisting' or 'co-operating' grace, in which Christ actively cooperates with us in doing what we do. Augustine's idea, as we shall see, was one of 'effecting' grace, in which Christ enters inside us and effects the whole matter himself. And although the idea of 'encouraging' grace is perfectly logical, there is no doubt, as Augustine realized, that it is a view which is open to serious criticism. It implies, for example, that if you are a *very* good competitor, a real natural at the sport, you may not need the coach's advice at all and you may be able to win the race or game or whatever by your own unaided power. 'Human beings can be without sin', said Pelagius, 'and can keep God's commandments, if they so wish.'[3] It could signify, too, that the most important aspect of Christ's incarnation was its exemplary and instructive quality—a model for us to imitate—and that his agony, death, resurrection, and ascension may not have been wholly necessary or, at least, not necessary in quite the same sense as the rest of the Christian Church defined necessity.

For Augustine, this was a denial of the basic principle of Christianity. It was a degradation of grace and an insult to the Son of God. Christ became incarnate to save *all* people, not just most, and, in Augustine's view, there were innumerable passages in Saint Paul which made it abundantly clear that grace was not, emphatically not, something given

---

3. Pelagius, quoted by Augustine in *De gestis Pelagii,* 20.

to us simply to help us do more easily what we can naturally do by ourselves. Grace is something which must be given to us if we are to do anything good at all. Without it we cannot do a single good act, and without it, as a consequence, we are doomed. Let us now consider Augustine's arguments and see how he arrives at this conclusion.

Since Adam was our first parent, said Augustine, all of us existed potentially in him. We did not exist in him in physical bodily form, but in potentiality; there was no other source from which we could have come save from the loins of Adam. Therefore, since we all existed potentially in Adam, where Adam went, we went, and what Adam did, we did. And since Adam sinned, so we all sinned in Adam, and Saint Paul says so: 'Through one man sin entered this world, and through sin, death, and thus death passed on to all people, for *in him* all sinned' (Rom 5:12). To be precise, this is Augustine's reading of the Latin translation of this verse from Paul's letter to the Romans. The original Greek simply says, 'and thus death passed on to all people *because* all sinned'. But the misleading Latin translation does not in any way affect Augustine's logic. It simply reinforces it.

Since we all fell 'in Adam', so we are what Adam was in consequence: fallen, damned, doomed, condemned. At birth the whole human race is simply *una massa peccati*, 'one lump of sin',[4] and because we are so totally, so hopelessly corrupted, we can no more do good of our own power than a blind man can see, or someone with no legs get up and walk. It is just impossible. 'Of our own power', said Augustine, 'we can only fall.'[5] But how is this original taint transmitted? How is the sin and guilt of Adam actually communicated to us? How did we catch the disease?

Augustine's answer was that it comes with the act of sexual intercourse. Again, his thought is logical. Sexual intercourse naturally involves lust. Lust, for Augustine (following Saint Paul), is a sin. Therefore sexual intercourse is inherently sinful. Even in marriage it is—in itself—sinful, but the marital situation ensures that the sinful-

---

4. Augustine of Hippo, *De diversis quaestionibus ad Simplicianum,* I, *quaestio* 2 *argumentum,* and §16.

5. Augustine of Hippo, *Enarratio in Psalmos,* 129.1.

ness of the act is automatically forgiven. This Augustinian idea, that the sexual drive and sexual intercourse are inherently evil, was to have an unfortunate effect on western Christian views of sex from the fifth century to the present day.

It follows, then, that since we are no more than walking, talking lumps of sin, God's grace is absolutely essential. It is not just useful, not just convenient, not just helpful, but *essential*. And since we are unable—not just unwilling—to do good, this grace can never be 'merited' or 'deserved'. We are no longer like the prodigal son in the parable: we *cannot* make the first move. We have been tied hand and foot, gagged, eyelids sewn shut, ears plugged, and buried up to our necks in the earth. We can do absolutely nothing unless God provides us with his grace (i.e., digs us up and cuts our bonds), and then directs our steps to heaven. Grace, therefore, is not something which helps us do better what we can already do ourselves, but something which enables us to do what is otherwise wholly outside the realm of human possibility.

To whom, then, is this grace made available? Answer: to whom God wills. How many of these fortunates are there? Answer: God knows! But in his great work *On the City of the God (De civitate Dei)* Augustine says that the number of those to whom grace will be made available is the same as the number of the angels who fell with Lucifer, so that the population of the heavenly Jerusalem will remain constant.[6] But why should I be chosen to receive this grace and not you (or vice-versa)? Answer: the decisions of God are inscrutable (Augustine is quoting Rom 11:33). But since God is by definition fair and just, what he does must also be fair and just, even if we cannot appreciate it. Which is no great comfort to those of us on our way to hell.

In other words, what we have here is the Augustinian doctrine of *predestination*, the doctrine which maintains that only those who are predestined to receive grace may be saved, and that all others are doomed. But what of the statement in the first letter to Timothy that 'God wishes *all* people to be saved' (1 Tim 2:4)? Does not this contradict the principle? No, says Augustine, it does not. What it

6. See Augustine of Hippo, *De civitate Dei*, 22.1.

means is that God wants all those who are so predestined to be saved, and that does not include everyone.

The views of Pelagius, of the eastern church in general, and of Augustine therefore represent the three possible ways in which human initiative may—or may not—operate. Pelagius held that we are born with a will absolutely free and totally untainted by Adam's sin; we therefore retain the possibility of achieving salvation by ourselves. The easterners held that we are born with a will corrupted by Adam's sin, but not so corrupted that we cannot do at least a few good actions. In response to these actions God makes his grace available, and in cooperation with this grace, and *only* in cooperation with this grace, we can achieve salvation. Augustine held that we are born with a soul completely corrupted by Adam's sin and, of our own power, cannot do any good action at all. Our salvation is therefore entirely in the hands of God, and if he does not make his grace available to us, there is absolutely nothing that we can do about it. Pelagian infants, we might say, are born with 20/20 vision; Greek infants are in need of spectacles; Augustinian infants are born blind.

What, then, can we say of free will? Does not the Augustinian doctrine effectively annihilate human freedom? Despite various subtle defences of the doctrine, there is no doubt that it does. A soul which has not received grace may have free will, but it cannot use it freely. It is so corrupted that it is free only to sin. It is just as if you put me in the middle of an open field and then built a six-foot wall immediately in front of me, and two other walls on my left and right. Do I still have free-will? Yes. Can I use it freely? No, because I can only move in one direction: backwards. As Augustine said, 'Of our own power we can only fall'.

After grace has been received, free-will may perhaps play a greater role in the Augustinian scheme, but even then there are problems. Our will may cooperate with God's will, but only after God (who knows all things) has so arranged matters that this is bound to occur. God knows in advance what stimulus or motive will bring about a particular action; he knows what action he wants to occur; and he arranges for the necessary stimulus or motive accordingly. But again, we are no more than puppets dancing to the tune of the Master Puppeteer. And it is no answer to say that our free will is most free when it is freely put into the service of the Creator, since (a) it cannot be put into his service unless he so determines; (b) it cannot be kept there unless he so arranges; and (c) if our will is entirely his will, it becomes problematical as to whether it can be called our will at all. These are undoubtedly complex matters, and there are no easy solutions, and although later Latin theologians, from the ninth century onwards, felt obliged to grapple with the problem, a consideration of these later attempts at elucidation is outside the realm of this present book.[7]

The sombre and pessimistic doctrine of Augustine—sombre and pessimistic, that is, if one is not one of the elect—was certainly not received with favour by all parties. To condemn Pelagius was one thing; to accept the views of Augustine was quite another. No church, eastern or western, was prepared to deny some taint or corruption from Adam's foolishness, and no church, eastern or western, was prepared to assert that we can be saved without grace. But to go to the other extreme and willingly embrace Augustinian predestinationism was a very different matter. The situation was made worse by the fact that, as the years went by and the controversy dragged on, Augustine's statements on the question became more and more radical, and even his own supporters began, in many cases, to shy away from his inexorable logic.

Others were more outspoken in their opposition. Julian (d. 454), for example, the Pelagian bishop of Eclanum (a town near Benevento in southern Italy, now called Mirabella), objected on a number of grounds to what he regarded as Augustine's illogical, unbiblical, and unchristian pessimism.

First of all, Julian maintained that Augustine's view of the irresistible power of predestined grace left no place for the operation of human free will, and we cannot deny that he has a point. Furthermore, said Julian, it contradicts the statement in 1 Timothy 2:4 that God wants *everyone* to be saved, not just those he predestines.

Secondly, he objected profoundly to Augustine's view of the inherent sinfulness of sex. Genesis 1:25 states unequivocally that when

7. See D. N. Bell, *Many Mansions. An Introduction to the Development and Diversity of Medieval Theology West and East* (Kalamazoo/Spencer, 1996) Chapter 17.

God viewed the whole of his creation, he saw that it was good. It does not say that it was all good except for the genitals. Jesus himself had male genitals, says Julian, but in his case they were perfectly controlled. As far as Julian was concerned, Augustine's idiosyncratic idea was no more than the result of his early attraction to Manichaeanism and an adolescent obsession with sex. And as for the idea that a perfectly good God could condemn an unbaptized baby who had committed no sin to eternal damnation, even if the infant's suffering would be as light as possible, that, for Julian, was simply iniquitous.

To all these arguments Augustine, naturally, had counter-arguments, though we cannot trace the details of the controversy here. It ended only with the death of Augustine in 430. But it is clear that Julian was not alone in his criticisms. Even among those who, on the whole, were favourable to Augustine, attempts were made to mitigate the rigours of his doctrine. In certain monasteries of southern France, for example, competent thinkers such as John Cassian (c. 360–after 430) and Vincent of Lérins (d. before 450) came up with a compromise which, much later, would be termed 'Semi-Pelagianism', and which, in its essentials, was much the same as the position accepted by the eastern churches: namely, that though grace was essential for salvation, humanity had not totally lost its ability for good as a consequence of Adam's sin.

These 'semi-Pelagian' ideas proved popular, and they were widely accepted in certain parts of France and Britain for about a century. But there was always the problem that the reputation of Augustine was growing so rapidly in the west that to criticize him was like criticizing God's private secretary. Furthermore, opposing Augustine could easily be mistaken for supporting Pelagianism, and Pelagianism had been condemned again and again by the Church from the early fifth century onwards. It had been condemned at Carthage and Mileve in 416, condemned by Pope Innocent I in 417, condemned again at Carthage in 418, condemned at the Council of Ephesus—the third Ecumenical Council—in 431, condemned at the second council of Orange (together with 'Semi-Pelagianism') in 529, and it then gradually disappeared during the course of the sixth century. As a consequence of these councils, the Church declared (1) that Adam was not created mortal, but became mortal through sin (the Pelagians maintained that Adam was mortal from the start); (2) that everyone has been contaminated in some way by Adam's fall; (3) that God's grace is not available only for the forgiveness of sins already committed, but is necessary to prevent us from committing further sins; and (4) that grace does not simply enable us to do more easily what we can already do of our own free will. In other words, a person in whom God's grace operates is different in kind, not just in degree, from a person in whom grace is not to be found.

In the west, the Augustinian view triumphed. It is true that certain of the more rigorous aspects of his doctrine were quietly set aside— no western theologians until John Calvin much cared for hard-line predestinationism; but the Augustinian view of the utter corruption of human nature and the essentiality of grace came to dominate western moral theology. In the east, the situation was different. The Pelagian controversy had been primarily a western controversy—it had been conducted almost entirely in Latin, not Greek—and although the eastern bishops were aware of what was going on, they were, with a few exceptions, spectators rather than players. The condemnation of Pelagianism at Ephesus in 431 was a condemnation of Pelagius, not an endorsement of Augustine; and Augustine's views on the question of grace (written in Latin for a Latin audience) were read by few easterners, and had hardly any impact on eastern teaching. The Greek churches remained loyal to their more optimistic view, and have remained loyal to it ever since. Yet it must be clearly understood that although the eastern and western churches differed in their assessment of innate human depravity, they were entirely in agreement that salvation could not be achieved without grace, and they were likewise in agreement that the possibility of salvation was in some way intimately linked to the incarnation of the Son of God. But what was the precise nature of this linkage, and how was it that the life and death of one man could have such a profound effect upon the whole human race? It is to a consideration of this question and its various answers that we must now turn our attention.

This extraordinary sixth-century mosaic might also be entitled 'the Triumph of the Cross', for it shows the cross (with a tiny face of Christ in the centre) triumphant over a restored creation. The garden we see is the Garden of Eden before the Fall, and the Garden of Paradise yet to come. The figure beneath the cross is Saint Apollinaris (not the heretic we met in Chapter Eight but the saint to whom the church is dedicated), and to his left and right are twelve sheep symbolizing the twelve disciples. The transfigured Christ is accompanied by Moses and Elijah, and the three sheep to the left and right of the cross represent Peter, James, and John, the three disciples who were present at the Transfiguration. The hand of God emerges from the clouds at the very top of the scene, bestowing blessing.

THE TRANSFIGURATION

Location: Basilica of Sant' Apollinare in Classe, Ravenna, Italy
Photo: Terryl N. Kinder

XIII

CUR DEUS HOMO?

'WHY DID GOD BECOME HUMAN?', *Cur Deus Homo?*, is the title of a well-known treatise by Anselm, who was archbishop of Canterbury from 1093 to his death in 1109. It is a remarkable work, and in focussing attention on the question of just how redemption took place, the book gave rise to a great deal of theological speculation and not a few controversies. In the centuries after Anselm, we find in the west a mass of material on the subject, much of it carefully and systematically presented, but in the centuries with which we are here concerned this is not the case. The question was asked—of course it was—but the detail, comprehensiveness, and systematic presentation which we find in and after the Middle Ages is not to be found in the earlier period.

Furthermore, it is not a question which can be answered simply. To ask why God became human is to ask the reason for his birth, life, teaching, betrayal, death, resurrection, and ascension, and it may well be that no one answer will suffice. It's like asking people why they have a particular job. There may be a number of reasons: they enjoy the work, they feel a need to get out of the house, they like their fellow-workers, or they need the money. All these may be true, but all combine together, and at any one time one reason may be more relevant than another. Similarly, we do not find, and should not expect to find, any one single answer to Anselm's question. There are instead a number of answers, and the theologians of the early Church use one at one time, another at another, and some or all may appear in juxtaposition in the same treatise or even on the same page. The best way of looking at the question, therefore, is to view the same Christ under four different aspects: Christ as Teacher and Model, Christ as Restorer, Christ as Victor, and Christ as Victim. Any one of these four aspects may be dominant at any one time, but no one excludes the others. There was, after all, only the one person of the incarnate Lord.

For the earliest writers—the Apostolic Fathers—Christ the Teacher and Model was of paramount importance. We have been called from darkness to light, says Clement of Rome, 'from ignorance to the knowledge of the glory of his name'.[1] Christ has revealed to us the truth, the whole truth, the perfect law, the way to salvation, the road to immortality, the paths of faith. The so-called second letter of Clement (which is neither a letter nor by Clement, but an anonymous early Christian sermon dating from perhaps 100 CE) is even clearer. How shall we gain our reward? By acknowledging him through whom we are saved. And how do we acknowledge him? 'By doing what he says and not disobeying his commandments.'[2] The Apostolic Fathers look to heaven rather than earth, and salvation for them is something which will happen in the future, at Christ's second coming, when all are judged according to their deserts, and those who have lived a life in accordance with Christ's example and

---

1. Clement of Rome, *To the Corinthians*, 59.2.
2. Clement 3:2-4.

Christ's teachings will be rewarded with everlasting bliss. They *say* that Christ was crucified for us and suffered for our sakes, and there is no doubt that they believed it. They say that he died for us and rose again. But what they say on these matters is, on the whole, formal and biblical, and they offer little evidence of really having thought about what the phrases mean. Even for the anti-docetic Ignatius, who (as we saw in Chapter Eight) was so insistent on the reality of Christ's humanity and the reality of his death, it is the imitation of Christ which is fundamental. 'Become imitators of Jesus Christ', he tells the Christians of Philadelphia, 'just as he was [an imitator] of his Father.'[3] Indeed, of all the early Christian writers, Ignatius is the most insistent on following in the footsteps of his divine teacher and exemplar. 'Give me leave', he says, 'to be an imitator of the suffering of my God.'[4] In fact, for the Apostolic Fathers in general, the way to salvation can be summarized as 'Do what Christ told you, do as Christ showed you, and you'll go to heaven.'

For the Apologists, too, Christ as Teacher was of great importance. This is hardly surprising when we remember that many of them were deeply involved with the threat of Gnosticism, that Gnosticism was the greatest danger to the early Church, and that Gnosticism was based on the principle of divine revelation. What is a Gnostic? Someone who *knows*. That knowledge has been revealed to them, and to them alone, in secret communications and esoteric instructions by a divine or semi-divine revealer. This, as we have seen, is something that the Apologists would not countenance for a moment. On the contrary, said they—especially Irenaeus of Lyons and Clement of Alexandria—the true Gnostic is the Christian, the true Teacher is Christ, and the True Gnosticism is the Christian tradition. It is only to be expected, therefore, that Christ the True Teacher, Christ the True Revealer, Christ the True Illuminator looms large in their writings.

Yet that is not all they have to say. Justin, for example, anticipates all the other answers we have noted above. He sees Christ as the Second Adam, restoring a creation which had been seriously damaged

3. Ignatius of Antioch, *To the Philadelphians*, 7.2.
4. Ignatius of Antioch, *To the Romans* 6.3.

by the sins of the First Adam. This is the theory of recapitulation which we discussed in Chapter Eight (Irenaeus, who perfects the doctrine, properly credits Justin with the idea) and it involves both Christ as Restorer and Christ as Victor. Justin recognized that in his life and death, Christ has overcome the devil and his demons and has removed us from their grasp, and he sees the cross as the chief symbol of his power. Nor is he in any doubt that Christ suffered for us, took our sins upon himself, and died that we might be forgiven: all these are ideas which, as we shall see, involve both Christ as Victor and Christ as Victim. But in the writings of Justin, these concepts appear only in their infancy. He does not develop them at length—we would hardly expect him to do so, given his time and his intentions—and their elaboration and refinement were to be the work of later generations of Christian theologians.

Christ as Restorer is a particularly Platonic idea. The principle is simple. When he became human, Christ took upon himself true and complete human nature. By taking this human nature upon himself, he transformed it and sanctified it. And by this transformation and sanctification, human nature, which had been rendered corruptible and mortal by the Fall, once again became capable of incorruption and immortality. And why is this idea particularly Platonic? Because Platonists prefer to think in terms of abstract universals rather than concrete particulars. They are happier dealing with 'Chairness' than with particular chairs, and would rather discuss 'The Cat' or 'Catness' than a particular feline called Rumbelow or Shinsilver. We discussed this in Chapter Two. For the Platonists, therefore, it was more natural to see the incarnation as the uniting of universal divinity with universal humanity, rather than the uniting of God with the individual Jesus, the Galilean son of Mary.

When we consider that the Platonic outlook was characteristic of virtually all Greek theologians from Justin Martyr onwards, we will appreciate just how important and widespread was the idea of Christ the Restorer. But when we consider that in the west Platonism was always less dominant, and eventually—in the later Middle Ages—was superseded by the views of Aristotle, who preferred particulars to universals, dogs to 'Dogness', we will appreciate that the western emphasis was bound to be rather different.

The principle of Christ as Restorer lies at the root of the most important eastern concept of human development: the idea of deification (*theōsis* in Greek). Athanasius put the matter in a nutshell: 'God became human that in him humans might become god'.[5] But what does it mean 'to become god', to be 'deified'? For the Christian Church, it did not mean that human beings could be identified with their Creator. That was never countenanced. We cannot become God. What it meant is that we can become 'what God is'. That is to say, we have the capacity to experience and share—the technical term is 'participate'—in the *attributes* or *qualities* of God, and the most important of these attributes or qualities are his blessedness, incorruption, and immortality. Before the Fall, Adam and Eve participated in all these things. After they were expelled from Eden they lost that participation, they became sinful, corrupt, and mortal, and they passed on that sinfulness, corruption, and mortality to all their descendants. With the incarnation, Christ has restored to us the possibility of participation, and as a consequence of his life and sacrificial death, humanity is now, once again, capable of participating in the divine nature.

The key to this idea, as we said above, is Platonism and, above all, the Platonic preference for speaking in terms of universals rather than particulars. Thus, when we refer to the First and Second Adam, we are not so much talking about the man Adam and Jesus the son of Mary as about Humanity Then and Humanity Now. With the disobedience and sinfulness of the First Adam, 'humanity' fell. With the obedience and sinlessness of the Second Adam—Christ—'humanity' was restored. The restoration was not restricted to Jesus alone, but was communicated to the whole human race. In the incarnation, God became *human*, not just a particular human being, and he has therefore restored to all of us what all of us lost with Adam's fall.

For the eastern Church, then, the possibility of deification is one of the greatest gifts of the incarnation. As the first sin separated humanity from God, so the incarnation restored the relationship. Christ, as God-made-human, united in his own being divinity and humanity and, as both God and man, could restore the flow of grace and offer

5. Athanasius, *Ad Adelphium*, 4.

us once again the possibility of participation in the divine attributes. We can once again be blessed, incorrupt, and immortal, but whereas the process may begin here on earth, it can find its fulfilment only in the world to come. Only there can we participate fully in the incorruptibility and immortality of our Creator.

This is certainly an impressive and optimistic doctrine, yet it gives rise to two important questions. First of all, is the restoration brought about in and through Christ an automatic and universal restoration? That is to say, does everyone benefit from it, whether pagan or Christian, saint or sinner, whether they want to or not? And secondly, if restoration was effected simply by the entry of Christ into the world, what need was there for his death and resurrection?

The answer to the first question is that the *possibility* of divinization is indeed offered to all, but not all will take advantage of it. Who will take advantage? For western Augustinians, those who are predestined to do so. For easterners, non-Augustinians, and heretical Semi-Pelagians, those who, by their own free will, in cooperation with grace, choose to do so. And since grace normally operates only within the Church (we shall discuss this matter in our next chapter), the effects of restoration and re-creation are, in practice, limited to Christians. 'Outside the Church there is no salvation',[6] said Augustine (echoing Cyprian of Carthage), and no Christian at the time would have disagreed with him.

The answer to the second question—why did Christ need to die and rise again?—becomes clear once we remember that not only are we subject to disease and corruption as a consequence of Adam/humanity's sin, but we are also doomed to die. 'Dust you are,' said God to Adam, 'and to dust you shall return' (Gen 3:19). Thus, because we all share in the sin of Adam and have ourselves sinned from Eden onwards, we are all under sentence of death. Humanity sinned; humanity has been condemned; humanity must die. And humanity *did* die. But it was not we who died: it was the Second Adam. It was Christ, the *New* Humanity, who bore our sins, paid our debt, released us from God's condemnation, and thereby enabled us

---

6. Augustine of Hippo, *De baptismo*, IV.xvii. 24.

to benefit from the effects of his restoration. The Platonist viewpoint is here essential: Christ on the cross is not just Jesus, the son of Mary. He is, in a sense, humanity itself. We-in-Christ achieve immortality as we-in-Adam were rendered mortal. Hence Athanasius's statement: 'God became human that *in him* humans might become god.' The death of Christ enables us to benefit from Christ's transformation of humanity, but if Christ had not died, if Christ had not paid our debt, the process could not even begin. If we may use a modern analogy, Christ, the God-man, was the only one who could reconnect the broken cables and restore the current which once flowed between human beings and God. But since he could reconnect them only in and through his own body, and since the current was so powerful, he had to die in order to achieve his goal.

The crucifixion, then, was wholly necessary if we were to be released from sin and death—the Fathers were agreed on that—but just how was the release accomplished? What precisely happened in those agonizing hours when the Second Adam died? Let us consider the answer of Gregory of Nyssa. According to Gregory, Adam sinned of his own free will, and, as a consequence, it was by its own free will that humanity fell into the clutches of Satan. The devil therefore has certain rights over us, and, as we saw a moment ago, could justly demand our deaths. This, however, was not in accordance with God's plan, so he determined to deceive the devil. In place of humankind he offered him instead his own incarnate Son, and when Satan saw Jesus in all his perfection and power and sinlessness, he decided that the exchange would be much to his advantage, and he agreed. But unfortunately for Satan, he had not realized that concealed under the robe of flesh was the second person of the Trinity, true God, consubstantial with the Father, omnipotent, omniscient, eternal, unchangeable, and immortal. Or, using Gregory's own somewhat unpleasing metaphor: the greedy fish (the devil) gulped down the bait of the flesh and found himself caught on the hook of the Divinity.[7]

When this happened, all hell broke loose (this is a nice opportunity to use the phrase literally). Christ the Victorious Victim conquered

7. See Gregory of Nyssa, *Oratio catechetica*, 24.

death, which, of course, had no hold over God. He descended into hell, where he preached to the 'spirits in prison' (1 Pet 3:19), and overthrew the power of the demons, binding the devil hand and foot. The ransom for humanity was paid; death was overthrown; Satan was deceived, conquered, and bound; and from the depths of hell Christ arose triumphant.

This theory of the devil's deception was not new with Gregory. Traces of it can be found far back in the second century, and it is perfectly clear in the work of Origen, whom Gregory esteemed. Yet Gregory's imagery of bait and hook was not to everyone's taste—in his *Cur Deus homo?* Anselm rejects it—and the whole theory of deceiving the devil raised two important questions. First, whether the transaction was ethical; and second, whether the devil really had any rights at all.

Theologians in the centuries after Gregory therefore found it necessary to amend the scheme. They were in no doubt that the human race had sinned and that, as a consequence, it had put itself in Satan's power. But Satan, instead of just sitting back and counting souls, decided to help things along by intervening actively in the matter: he seduced Judas and assailed Jesus. But since Jesus was actually sinless, any assault on him was contrary to divine law, and Satan had thereby overreached himself. Because he had gone beyond his permitted bounds, he was therefore just as guilty as humankind; and because he had abused his powers, whatever happened to him was just and right and proper. And as to whether he had rights, the Fathers were, on the whole, agreed: he did have rights, but only because God permitted him to have them.

However ethical or unethical was the theory of the devil's deception, the later Fathers never lost sight of the event which lay at the heart of the matter: the death of Christ. Christ was the ransom, the sacrifice, the substitute; and according to Gregory of Nazianzus (and a host of others), when he was crucified, our sins were crucified with him. This was not just a formal acknowledgement of the fact. For these theologians the death of Christ was an event of real and momentous significance, and when Basil the Great says that the price for all humanity was paid in 'the holy and most precious blood of our Lord Jesus Christ',[8] he really means what he says. Despite their concern with restoration and deification, the later eastern theologians never lost sight of this crucial event, and despite a tendency to conceal the cross by a wealth of elaborate symbolism and emphasis on the Resurrection, they never denied the necessity of the bloody sacrifice which took place upon it.

The importance of the crucifixion—of Christ as Victim—was, however, more marked in the west. We have already seen that Tertullian regarded it as the central event of Christianity, and that in his view it contained within itself the whole essence of the Christian tradition. It was he, too, who introduced the term 'satisfaction'—*satisfactio* in Latin—and although he himself did not use the word with reference to the work of Christ (Cyprian of Carthage may have been the first to do so, and his approach is tentative and cautious), later Latin writers (including Anselm) welcomed it as the best expression for the payment of the penalty due to God because of human sin. This is not to deny that the other aspects we have considered also played a role in western theology. Christ as Teacher was of great importance for Clement of Rome (whom we met in Chapter Three) as well as for Tertullian. Christ as Restorer and 'Deifier' was not neglected, although this aspect of his work is elaborated more by those who, like Hilary, the bilingual bishop of Poitiers (the 'Athanasius of the West' whom we mentioned in Chapter Seven), were deeply influenced by the world of Alexandria and Constantinople. And the theory of the devil's deception enjoyed widespread popularity. But it was above all on Christ as Victim that western theology concentrated:

> He died that we might be forgiven,
> He died to make us good,
> That we might go at last to heaven,
> Saved by his precious blood.

This famous Victorian hymn (written by Cecil Frances Alexander) is the authentic voice of the Latin west, and the western answer to

8. Basil of Caesarea, *Homilia in Psalmum* 48.3.

the question 'Why did God become human?' could well be 'Because he had to die'. To some extent this is a simplification of the more metaphysical theories of the Greek east, and it is an easy doctrine to understand. We are guilty; we are condemned to death; someone else pays the price ('It is a far, far better thing that I do . . .'); the price is accepted; we are released. This, as we saw in Chapter Seven, was the thought of Tertullian, and it also reflects the thought of a long line of formulators of western doctrine who were more often hard-headed administrators than speculative theologians. On the other hand, as the genius of Augustine makes clear, this is not all that the west had to say. He, as usual, was able to perceive and draw together all the threads we have so far considered and to weave them into a comprehensive and coherent whole.

Augustine never forgets Christ as Teacher, but he is a teacher who teaches more by his example than by his words. As the living embodiment of love, he shows us how to love. And as the most as-tonishing example of humility (this is *God*, after all, who has emptied himself and become human), he teaches us how to be humble. Ac-cording to Augustine, there are three steps on the path which leads to redemption: the first step is humility; the second step is humility; and the third step is humility.[9]

Nor does he forget Christ as Restorer, but his approach to this aspect is more typically western than eastern. He does indeed say that God became human to make us humans gods, but that is not where his real interest lies. His Restorer is the Mediator, the one true Mediator, who, because he is truly God and truly human, brings God down to us and raises us up to God. In his own person, Christ bridges the gap which Adam opened, and restores God and humanity to its right relationship. This is the atonement in the literal sense: the restored 'at-one-ment' of the Creator and his creation.

We also see in his work copious examples of Christ as Victor over the devil and his demons. But Augustine is well aware that the idea was problematical, and although he sometimes uses imagery similar to that of Gregory of Nyssa (Satan, he says, was caught by the lure

9. Augustine of Hippo, *Epistola* 118.iii.22.

of Christ's body like a mouse 'taking the bait in a mousetrap'[10]), his own view of the matter is subtly different. When humanity sinned, it certainly passed into the power of the devil, but this does not mean that the devil had any absolute rights. He was *permitted* by God to take us into his power. But because he had no rights in the matter, neither could he demand any ransom; and what this means, in turn, is that the death of Christ was not, in itself, any payment made to the devil. With his death, the Second Adam—Christ—restored the creation which had been deformed by the First Adam, and once again united Creator and creation. In this the devil had no say. He may not have liked it, but there was nothing he could have done about it. The crucifixion released the souls he had in his care whether he liked it or not, and for all his anger and fury, he could not have prevented them from walking out of his domain through the door which Christ had opened. God, however, is a just God, and to give the devil no choice in the matter seemed not consonant with divine justice. So God delivered up his Son to death, and the devil, in his greed and malice, could not resist reaching out and taking him. And then, because he had taken a sinless victim, the devil himself was caught. He had overstepped his appointed bounds, and he was therefore as sinful and guilty as the human souls he had in his care. 'Right,' said God, 'in payment for *your* sin, I require the return of humanity', and Satan had no choice but to deliver it up.

In other words, it was the crucifixion itself, not any ransom paid to the devil, which brought about our release, remission, and redemption, and the 'deception' of the devil only resulted in his being required by divine law to do something which he would have had to do anyway. It is the crucifixion itself which is central for the western Augustine. 'By his death,' he says, 'the one most true sacrifice offered for us, Christ purged, abolished, extinguished whatever guilt there was by which the principalities and powers (i.e., the demons) were justly holding us fast to pay its penalty.'[11] Nor is this an isolated passage, and with the ideas and authority of Tertullian and Augustine at

---

10. Augustine of Hippo, *Sermo* 261.1.
11. Augustine of Hippo, *De Trinitate*, 4.13.17.

its source and as its foundation, the idea that Christ is the Victorious Victim, not surprisingly, came to represent the dominant strain of western thinking on the redemption.

It is clear, however, that neither in the east nor the west do we have four separate theories as to how salvation works. There are not four separate answers to the question '*Cur Deus Homo?*' Christ as Teacher, Restorer, Victor, and Victim is one and the same Christ, and although the emphases change, all four factors interact and concur. East and west, naturally, stress different aspects. Why should they not? They represent, after all, different peoples with different cultures, different languages, and different outlooks. But neither denied or wished to deny that the whole of Christ's life was necessary, and that his birth, teaching, example, death, resurrection, and ascension were all alike essential for the fulfilment of the divine plan. We are redeemed by the *whole* of his incarnation, not just by one single part of it, and by God's grace we are able to enjoy all the benefits of this redemption. We must now turn, therefore, to a consideration of just how these benefits may be obtained, and where they are most effectively to be found. In other words, we must turn from a discussion of the incarnate body of Christ to a discussion of his mystical body, the Christian Church.

The first basilica was erected by Constantine the Great on the supposed site of the crucifixion of Saint Peter. Begun between 326 and 333, the building took about thirty years to complete, and was a splendid five-aisled basilica, some four hundred feet in length. By the fifteenth century, however, it was in a state of disrepair, and plans were made for a new Saint Peter's. The first stone of the present basilica was laid on 18 April 1506, but it took more than a century for the building to be completed.

OLD SAINT PETER'S BASILICA, ROME

by Domenico Tasselli (sixteenth century)
Location: Saint Peter's Basilica, Vatican State
Photo: Scala / Art Resource, New York

XIV

ONE AND HOLY:
THE MYSTICAL BODY OF CHRIST

THE CHURCH WAS ALWAYS CONVINCED that it was the receptacle of grace and, without wishing to limit the omnipotence of God, it was equally convinced that under normal circumstances, salvation was not to be found outside it. Cyprian, the third-century bishop of Carthage, put the matter in a nutshell: 'Someone who does not have the Church as mother cannot have God as father'.[1] Augustine, likewise, was not in doubt: 'Outside the Church there is no salvation'.[2] He knew that exceptions did occur—there was the obvious case of the centurion Cornelius in Acts 10—but such exceptions were very

1. Cyprian of Carthage, *De unitate ecclesiae*, 6.
2. See Chapter Thirteen, n. 6.

rare. If the normal, visible means of grace were available, the believer was expected to use it. The Church was not just a convenient, but a *necessary*, part of the process of salvation. It was not just a social group, a society of believers; it was the mystical body of Christ. This was a concept of first importance for all the Fathers, both eastern and western, for as Christ united himself with our humanity in the incarnation, so we are united with him and with one another as members of his mystical body. As members of the Church we are incorporated—the word means literally 'put into the body'—into Christ, and as Christ himself is eternal and indestructible, so, too, is his mystical body. As Christ fulfilled the promises of the Old Testament, so also is his mystical body the fulfilment of those promises: it is the true Israel, the eschatological society, and, as we are told in the so-called 'Constantinopolitan' Creed, it is one, holy, universal, and apostolic.

But what, exactly, do these terms mean, and how can they be defended as descriptions of a Church which was continually racked by heresy and schism, which was often led by men of mixed motives and devious designs, and which, on many occasions, did not appear to be particularly holy?

Let us begin by considering the Church in its oneness, for this will lead us in turn to a discussion of its holiness, universality, and apostolic nature. At the most obvious level, since Christ has only one body, so there can be only one Church. And if there is only one Church, there can be—or should be—only one baptism into the one body, one faith in the one Lord, and one belief in the one God. And since Christ united himself with us because of his love for us, so it is love which unites us with him and ourselves with each other: 'We love, because he first loved us' (1 Jn 4:19). The Church is one in mutual love, said Augustine, love is its life-blood. But he was not the first to say this, and the idea has a history going right back to the New Testament.

What, then, are we to say of the heretics and schismatics? By separating themselves from the Church (the schismatics), or by denying its teaching (the heretics), they have imperilled both its unity and its universality and have turned their backs on the vessel of grace. But are we to regard such people in exactly the same light as pagans, Jews, Zoroastrians, Gnostics, and other perverted unfortunates? Putting it another way, is there any difference between a person who has never known or been associated with Christianity, and a person who was born into a Christian family, was baptized, attended church regularly, but then, because (let us say) they found Pelagianism more attractive than orthodoxy, found themselves outside the Christian fold in their attempt to live a Christian life? There were two answers to the question—one more rigorous, one more liberal.

Let us consider the case of Novatian. Born about 200, Novatian was an intelligent and acute theologian, the author of an excellent, orthodox, and neglected treatise on the Trinity, and the chief presbyter of the Roman church. In the year 250, he and all other Christians found themselves subjected to a vicious persecution instigated by the emperor Decius, and during eighteen months of terror (which ended in June 251 with Decius's death), a considerable number of Christians had apostatized—that is to say, had denied Christianity and saved their lives by making the requisite offerings to the pagan gods. Many others, however, by simple bribery had been able to obtain from the civil authorities official documents called *libelli pacis* or 'peace booklets', which stated that they had sacrificed, when, in fact, they had not. What was to be done with these people once the persecution was over? Many of them, naturally, wished to return to the Church, and those who had simply bought the necessary documents—they were referred to as *libellatici*—could say, with some justification, that they had never really left it.

Novatian was at first fairly lenient and farsighted with regard to these individuals, but then, partly because of his own austere theology, but mainly because of his determined opposition to and dislike of Pope Cornelius I (who was also lenient, but who had been elected in April 251 to the position Novatian himself had coveted), he joined the more rigorous party which maintained that once you were out of the Church, you were out forever, and that there was no possible way back in. Novatian then had himself consecrated as an anti-pope to Cornelius, and the Novatianist sect spread rapidly and achieved considerable importance. Its organization was precisely the same as that of the 'official' Church, and with one exception its doctrinal teachings were identical. The only difference was that the Novatianists did not think that there was any forgiveness for major sins committed after baptism. For this belief they were excommunicated.

What we have here, then, are schismatics who are orthodox Christians in all matters but one. Are we really to consider them as no better than pagans? According to Cyprian of Carthage (d. 258), Novatian's contemporary, the answer to that question is Yes. So far as Cyprian was concerned, all those outside the Church were to be considered in precisely the same light, and there was no essential difference between a Novatianist schismatic and the emperor Decius himself. Furthermore, if any of the Novatianists had received baptism from Novatianist clergy, that baptism was invalid; and if any of these people eventually saw the light and expressed a desire to join the official, true, orthodox, universal Church—Cyprian's Church—then they would have to be properly baptized, or, in their eyes, re–baptized.

This point of view was thought by many to be far too harsh, and one of those who thought it too harsh was Pope Stephen I, who had ascended the papal throne in May 254. It was the more humane Roman practice to readmit those who had apostatized simply by giving them an appropriate penance (though we should note that at this time in the Church's history, such penance could be long and arduous, and we will say more on the matter in the next chapter), and to receive those who had been baptized by the Novatianists—or any other schismatic Christians—simply by giving them absolution by the laying on of hands. The great metropolitan see of Alexandria and most of the Palestinian Churches agreed with Rome in this matter, but North Africa (which was Cyprian's homeland and always had a hard-line tendency), Syria, and most of Asia Minor did not. Cyprian certainly did not. Like his predecessor Tertullian (whom he esteemed), he considered heretical baptism to be totally invalid, and was quite prepared to oppose the pope—or, more accurately, the Church of Rome—in saying so. As a consequence, the Church was faced with the threat of a major division, with the Romans and their allies on one side, and the North Africans and their allies on the other. That this split did not occur was a consequence not of diplomacy but of death. Stephen died in August 257 and Cyprian in September 258, and with the departure from the scene of the two principal protagonists, the situation gradually stabilized, though the issue itself remained unresolved. Most of the west accepted the idea that those baptized in heretical sects might be admitted to the 'true' Church by simple laying on of hands. Much of the east (especially Asia Minor), and, not surprisingly, North Africa, continued to demand rebaptism. But the dispute brings to light two very important questions: (1) what is the relationship of the Church of Rome and the other Churches, and (2) what makes a sacrament (such as baptism) valid?

Let us begin by examining the relationship of Rome to the rest of the Christian world. The Church had always believed that it was 'apostolic'. That is to say, it was sure that it was built on the foundation of the prophets and the apostles, and that the chief cornerstone was Christ himself (Eph 2:20). This was stressed particularly by the second-century writers in their struggle with Gnosticism—we discussed the case of Irenaeus of Lyons in Chapter Three—who insisted that the true tradition of the Church was to be found, not in secret gospels and esoteric teachings, but in the visible and public tradition handed down from Christ himself to his apostles, and from the apostles to their successors. Thus, Tertullian could say that although there were many great churches, they were all really the first Church, that which was founded by the apostles, and from which all others derived. 'In this way all are primitive and apostolic.'[3] Who, then, were the successors of the apostles? In the earliest Christian writings we find no clear distinction between the offices of presbyter/priest and bishop, but it was not long—certainly by the first half of the second century—before bishops, and bishops alone, were seen as the inheritors of the apostolic powers and responsibilities. It was for them (if we may use the terminology of a later age) to preach the gospel, govern the Church, and administer the sacraments. We see the beginnings of this idea in the writings of Ignatius of Antioch, who saw in the bishop the symbol of the Church's unity, and we see it very much more clearly in the letters and treatises of Cyprian of Carthage.

First of all, Cyprian had no doubt that each individual bishop was master in his own diocese, and that each individual bishop was

---

3. Tertullian, *De praescriptione haereticorum*, 20.

answerable to God alone. Secondly, he took the ideas of Ignatius much further and was prepared to state categorically that since the bishop is in the Church and the Church in the bishop, then if you are not with the bishop, you are not with the Church. Thirdly, the bishops together form a *collegium* or college (one might also translate the word as board or committee or council), and each individual member of this college enjoys the collective powers of the whole college. When any bishop speaks, therefore, he speaks with the authority of the whole apostolic Church behind him. What, then, of Rome?

The bishop of Rome, says Cyprian, is just like every other bishop, and he may therefore speak with this apostolic authority. But—and it is a very important but—no one is entitled to set himself up as a 'bishop of bishops' and force his colleagues to compulsory obedience. In other words, Cyprian is perfectly willing to ascribe to Rome a primacy of *honour*, but not a primacy of *jurisdiction*. If the bishops were to meet in synod, Rome might naturally take the chair, but when it came to the vote, the Roman vote would count no more and no less than any other vote, and if Rome were out-voted, Rome lost. A bishop is a bishop is a bishop, and no one bishop has any more or any less apostolic authority than any other.

The view of Rome was rather different. From an early period its bishops had assumed that they had a greater authority than that of other bishops, even though the other bishops had not been prepared to accept it. We saw in Chapter Three how Clement, at the very end of the first century, was quite prepared to remonstrate with the Church at Corinth; and late in the second century, Pope Victor I (pope from 189 to 198) had tried to impose his will on the Churches of Asia Minor who celebrated Easter on the precise day of the Jewish Passover and not (as was the Roman practice) on the Sunday following. He did not succeed, that is true, but his attempt shows clearly that in Victor's view, Rome had a perfect right to intervene in the affairs of another diocese.

Pope Stephen, Cyprian's adversary, wholly agreed with this, and based his claim on the famous Petrine text in Matthew 16:18: 'You are Peter, and on this rock I will build my Church'. He was the first pope we know of who did so. And despite the fact that Cyprian and a large number of bishops like him disagreed radically with this concept (many at the time— and afterwards—interpreted the 'rock' not as Peter, but as Peter's faith), it gradually gained wider and wider acceptance in the west, especially through the efforts of popes like Damasus I and Innocent I.

Damasus (pope from 366 to 384) had a reputation for enjoying the good life, but he was also determined to uphold the purity of Christian doctrine. He was therefore particularly active in suppressing heresy, both eastern and western, but he neither trusted nor understood the Greek mind. It is significant, for example, that he took no part at all in the Second Ecumenical Council in 381. Furthermore, Damasus was convinced (like Stephen) that he was the true successor of Saint Peter, and that conciliar decisions, especially with regard to creeds, were valid only if they were approved by the pope. This claim is important, for it indicates a new approach to papal power. Hitherto, it had been the Church of Rome, not the individual bishop of Rome, who claimed the right to intervene in the affairs of other Churches. But with Damasus, we see a transition from *Roman* authority to *papal* authority, and it was a transition happily endorsed by Innocent I.

Innocent (pope from 402 to 417) was an extraordinarily talented man of great ability, and he had no hesitation in claiming more power for the papacy than any of his predecessors. In his view, for example, any disputed matters of faith—if they were sufficiently serious—should be submitted to the see of Peter for judgement, and there was no question but that the 'Roman custom' (especially in matters of liturgy) should prevail.

The ideas of Damasus and Innocent found their fulfilment in the second half of the fifth century, when Leo I the Great (pope from 440 to 461) took all the principles which had developed thus far, melded them together, added a certain amount of further material, and produced a cohesive doctrine of the Roman primacy which was to become the accepted viewpoint of the western Church until the Second Vatican Council in the 1960s. It is commonly referred to as the 'Leonine Doctrine of the Roman Primacy'. According to Leo, supreme authority was given to Peter by Christ, and Peter was the first bishop of Rome. This supreme authority is therefore transmitted only to those who succeed him as bishops of Rome, and the authority of other bishops is transmitted to them from

Christ *through* Peter, and not from Christ directly. Hence, whereas the authority of other bishops is limited to their own dioceses, the supreme authority of the bishop of Rome—*Petrus redivivus* or 'Peter alive again'— extends over the whole Church, and the bishop of Rome is the ultimate source of authority and doctrine. By the same token, the universality of the Church could easily be discerned, for what could be a more obvious manifestation of this universality than the acknowledgement by all churches of a single source of authority, and the universal acceptance of the Roman standard?

These ideas, though eventually accepted by the western churches, were never accepted by those in the east. Their view was essentially that of Cyprian: one bishop, one vote. And although there was never any doubt that Rome was the first and most honourable see of Christendom, and that the bishop of Rome was *primus inter pares*, 'first among equals', the eastern Churches never ascribed to him—and never have ascribed to him—any more than a primacy of honour. It was inevitable, therefore, that sometime in the future, east and west would clash on this point, and clash they did; but the story of that collision, and how it came to play a major role in the Great Schism of 1054, is a matter outside the scope of this present survey.[4]

Let us now turn to the second problem which arose from the dispute between Stephen and Cyprian: the question of the validity of the sacraments. To understand this—and its ultimate resolution—we must investigate yet another controversy: that of the Donatists.

Donatism began in North Africa in 311, with the disputed consecration of a new bishop of Carthage. The new bishop was named Caecilian, and his consecration was disputed for two reasons.

First, the whole business had been rushed, and the bishops of Numidia (roughly the area of modern Algeria) were not able to be present at the consecration. But the chief bishop of Numidia had the privilege of consecrating every bishop of Carthage, and, according to the Numidians and their supporters, a consecration without the Numidian primate was no consecration at all.

---

4. See D. N. Bell, *Many Mansions. An Introduction to the Development and Diversity of Medieval Theology West and East* (Kalamazoo–Spencer, 1996) 47–56.

Secondly, one of the bishops who consecrated Caecilian—Felix of Apthugni/Aptunga—had been caught up in the persecution of the emperor Diocletian, and was suspected of being a *traditor* or 'traitor [to the faith]'—i.e., someone who had saved his skin by surrendering copies of the Scriptures to the pagan authorities. Felix, we might add, was later acquitted of this charge, but before that occurred his opponents had no hesitation in accusing him of apostasy and betraying the faith. As an apostate, therefore, Felix was outside the Church, his episcopal rank was forfeit, and his presence at Caecilian's consecration must certainly invalidate the whole rite. As a consequence of all this, Caecilian was deposed, and a Carthaginian cleric called Maiorinus elected in his place. Maiorinus, however, did not live long to enjoy his episcopacy, and on his death he was succeeded by the much more formidable Donatus, after whom the heresy is named.

The Donatists were rigorists. In many ways they were similar to the austere Novatianists, and their hero was Cyprian. They explicitly denied the validity of sacraments celebrated by unworthy ministers (they were thinking especially of apostates), and they insisted that the Church, the body of Christ and the bride of Christ, should be preserved spotless, pure, and immaculate, and that its holiness was to be found in the holiness of its individual members. On this score the Donatists were the Puritans of the early Church, demanding perfection of all the faithful, and asserting, in consequence, that sinners were not part of the Church. Their views were condemned by their Roman rivals, but the schismatics persisted and grew in strength, partly because they claimed Cyprian as their main authority (and Cyprian was highly regarded in North Africa), and partly because they fed on anti-Roman North African nationalism which at the time could arouse very violent emotions.

Opposition to Donatism came first from Optatus, a fourth-century North African bishop of whose life we know nothing whatever, and then, more importantly, from Augustine, who developed the ideas of Optatus and established a number of extremely important principles. First of all, asked Augustine (and Optatus), who effects the sacraments, who makes them work? It is certainly not the officiating presbyter. Baptism, for example, is administered in the name of the Father, Son, and Holy Spirit, not in the name of John Smith or Bishop Donatus.

And neither John Smith nor Bishop Donatus, of their own power, is capable of transforming bread into flesh or wine into blood. No, it is *God* who effects the sacraments, and the officiating minister is no more than a channel for divine grace. For someone dying of thirst, it matters little whether the person who carries them water is clean or dirty: the essential thing is not the bearer, but the water. Similarly, because the author of any sacrament is not the officiating minister but the omnipotent God, then if the sacrament is celebrated in accordance with the tradition of the Church, the worthiness or unworthiness of the minister is wholly irrelevant. Indeed, if this were not the case, we could be in deep trouble. How do you know whether or not a priest is in a state of serious sin? And if you cannot be sure of this (and the priest is hardly going to tell you), then you cannot ever be sure of whether the sacrament is valid or whether it is not. And to have the validity of any sacrament dependent on a totally unknown quantity is a ridiculous and intolerable situation.

So is there any difference at all between baptism performed by, say, a Novatianist or Donatist, and baptism performed by the pope? Yes and No, says Augustine, for we need to distinguish a sacrament asleep from a sacrament awake. Or, in theological terms, we need to distinguish the *validity* of a sacrament from its *efficacy*. A baptized Donatist has truly been baptized, but the gift of baptism is dormant or sleeping. For it to awake and bring about all the effects which baptism does bring about (re-birth into the true body of Christ, washing off of past sins, communication of grace—matters we shall consider in our next chapter), the Donatist must leave Donatism and seek entry into the 'true' Church. Once there, the sacrament 'works' or wakes up or becomes effective, for only in the one true Church, the one body of Christ, is salvation to be found. With this theory Augustine produced a neat compromise between the Roman and North African positions: schismatic sacraments are valid, but not efficacious. Because they are valid, they do not need to be repeated (which agrees with Pope Stephen), but because they are not efficacious, their recipient, if he or she remains outside the Church, is still doomed (which agrees with Cyprian).

Furthermore, for those who join the universal Church, and for those already in it, salvation is offered freely. But to whom is it offered, asks Augustine? Listen to Saint Paul: 'Christ Jesus came into the world to save sinners' (1 Tim 1:15). He did not come to save the perfect. The Donatists' view of the holiness of the Church is therefore utterly wrong. The Church is not a society of saints, but a school for sinners. It is a Noah's ark (the analogy is an old one) in which are to be found all manner of beasts, both clean and unclean. As far as Augustine was concerned, the holiness of the Church was not to be found in the holiness of its individual members, but in the holiness of the holy grace which was mediated through its sacraments. Its holiness, therefore, was not something created by and dependent on its human members, but something bestowed upon it by its divine Lord. It was an *objective*, not a *subjective* holiness.

On the other hand, Augustine could not deny that there was some truth in the Donatist claim that the Body and Bride of Christ should be as pure as possible, and, as a consequence of his intimate familiarity with Later Platonic thought and its clear-cut distinction of the ideal from the actual, he was able to accommodate this idea within his own doctrine. He therefore distinguished the essential, inner Church from the outward and visible Church. The former is composed of those individuals who are truly aflame with the fire of charity, who are filled with the Spirit of love—which is the Holy Spirit, the mutual love of Father and Son, as we saw in Chapter Seven—and who are utterly devoted to their Lord in body, soul, and spirit. It is these who are the Body of Christ in the true sense, and it is these who constitute the society of the saints. The others make up the visible Church—your average Christians, in other words—and although they are truly its members and although the sacraments are efficacious for them, they are, in a sense *in* the Church, but not *of* it. They are not the spiritual elite.

A little later, when Augustine had become deeply involved in the Pelagian controversy, he was able to add a refinement to this concept. The true, essential Church now becomes the company of the predestined, the society of the elect, and, accordingly, its number corresponds to the number of angels who fell with Satan.[5] This, of

5. See Chapter Twelve, n. 6.

course, reintroduces all the problems of predestinationism which we discussed briefly in Chapter Twelve, and if we take the idea to its logical conclusion, it raises the very nasty question of whether there is really any point to the visible and imperfect Church which is so important to so many Christians. Augustine, perhaps wisely, never pursues the theme, and the essential point of his argument is not the *identity* of the righteous saints, but the fact that they will not be known until the Last Judgement at the end of the world. Only then will the sheep be separated from the goats, and only God knows which is which. The Donatists, in trying to establish a sheep-only Church in this present time, are anticipating the Last Judgement, and claiming for themselves the sort of discrimination which belongs only to the Creator.

The essence of the Church, says Augustine, is not the outward holiness of its members, but the love they have for one another. Love, the Holy Spirit, is the life-blood of the Church—we said so at the beginning of this chapter—and you cannot be a member of the Church (and you cannot therefore be a true Christian) without truly loving God and your fellow Christians. His love, said Augustine, is something manifestly lacking among the Donatists, and the reason they are outside the Church is not their doctrinal inaccuracies or theological disagreements, but their lack of charity. We might observe, of course, that there was also a conspicuous lack of charity on the part of the anti-Donatist party, particularly after Augustine came to accept as valid the idea of coercion. This is the principle, based on Luke 14:23, that if the schismatics will not return to the one, true Church of their own free will, they may be forced to return, whether they want to or not. But given the nature of fallen humanity, this mutual lack of charity is, alas, not too surprising, and, until the Vietnam War, it was generally accepted that only the enemy commits war crimes.

Western theology after Augustine had little to add to his doctrine of the Church. There was certainly a development in the idea of the Roman primacy, but in its essentials, Augustine's doctrine became the officially accepted teaching of the west. The Church was one in the love of God and one's neighbour; it was holy in the holy grace of the Holy Spirit; it dispensed valid sacraments regardless of the worthiness or unworthiness of the minister; it was the outward and visible form—the institutional form—of an essential inner Church; it included both sinners and righteous, who would be separated only at the Last Judgement; it was a Church whose teachings and traditions began with Christ and his apostles and were then transmitted from generation to generation by its bishops, the successors of the apostles; and, finally, outside of this Church there was no salvation. To this must be added the Leonine contribution—accepted only in the west—that the universality of the Church can be seen in the universal acknowledgement of Rome and its bishop as the seat and source of supreme authority.

In the orthodox east, the situation, as we might expect, was rather different. The controversies we have examined (Novatianism and Donatism) and nearly all the protagonists (Cyprian, Novatian, Donatus, Optatus, Tertullian, Stephen, Victor, Cornelius, Damasus, Innocent, Leo, Augustine) were western, and, as we have seen before, it is controversy which gives rise to doctrine. On these subjects, the easterners, therefore, tended to repeat old and well-established ideas—the Church as the True Israel, as the Bride of Christ, as the vessel of the Holy Spirit, and so on—and although it is possible to find all of Augustine's ideas (but not Rome's claim to primacy of jurisdiction) echoed by Greek writers, the eastern Church (or, more precisely, the eastern Church before the Great Schism of 1054) never produced—never needed to produce—a consistent and comprehensive ecclesiology. Its main focus of interest lay with the Church as the Body of Christ, with the incorporation of the faithful into this body, and, as a consequence, with their 'deification' or 'divinization'. How was this 'incorporation' achieved? Most especially through participation in the Eucharist, the most dramatic of the sacraments, and it is to this drama and its significance that we must now turn our attention.

This splendid early sixth-century mosaic appears in the dome of the Arian baptistery in Ravenna. Jesus appears beardless and naked, submerged up to his waist in the waters of the Jordan. John the Baptist, clothed in what appears to be a leopard skin, is baptizing him, while the dove, representing the Holy Spirit, descends from Heaven and sprays water from its beak onto the head of Christ. The seated figure on the left is the pagan river-god of the Jordan, depicted as a white-haired, bearded old man in a green cloak. His presence in the scene clearly indicates that, at this time, pagan elements were still to be found in Christianity.

THE BAPTISM OF CHRIST

Location: Arian Baptistery, Ravenna, Italy
Photo: Terryl N. Kinder

XV

THE COMMUNICATION OF GRACE

THE FATHERS OF THE CHURCH were universally convinced that in a sacrament or mystery (the former term is Latin; the latter, Greek) we have the outward and visible sign of an inward and spiritual grace. They might not have expressed the idea in quite these words, nor have been quite sure as to how the two realities were connected, but the principle was accepted by all parties. This is, however, a fairly broad principle, and could obviously be applied to a large number of visible signs. Devout repetition of a creed, for example, could be the audible sign of an inner faith, and this inner faith itself was a consequence of sanctifying grace. A creed, therefore, could be called a sacrament, and is so called by Augustine in the fifth century. Not until the latter half of the twelfth century do we find what was to become the standard and formal list of seven sacraments—Baptism, Confirmation, Eucharist, Penance, Unction, Ordination, Matrimony—which is still used by the Roman Church, and, after being borrowed from it at a still later date, of most of the eastern Churches as well.

Yet despite the broad significance of the term and the possibility of dozens of sacraments (one twelfth-century writer—Hugh of Saint-Victor—lists thirty), four came to be generally considered as outstanding in their importance: the inseparable combination of baptism and chrismation/confirmation, penance (particularly in the west), and, of course, the Eucharist. It is these which we will consider in this present chapter.

In baptism one dies to one's old life, one is buried with Christ, and one rises again from the tomb of the waters to a new life in and with one's Saviour. Just as the whole body is buried, so the whole body must be submerged, and it was not until the early Middle Ages—perhaps the first half of the eighth century—that the western Church began to adopt the practice of affusion or infusion, in which the water is poured only over the head of a child. The reason, it seems, was not theological, but physical health. The earlier Church insisted—and the eastern Churches still insist—that without total submersion (so far as is practicable) the symbolism—the outward 'sign'—is incomplete. Practically, of course, submersion was and is not always possible, and, strictly speaking, submersion must be distinguished from immersion. In the former case, the whole body of the candidate for baptism is submerged; in the latter, only part of his or her body is immersed (perhaps up to the knees or waist), and the baptismal water poured over the rest. Sometimes, in the case of a baby, the infant is held in the priest's arms, and water poured over the baby's whole body. But in both cases—submersion and immersion—the essential principle remains the same: the candidate for baptism dies, is buried, and is raised up with Christ.

As a consequence of this baptismal rebirth, four things were thought to occur: Christ was accepted as Saviour; one entered the ark of salvation, the universal Church; one's previous sins were washed away; and one received the grace of the Holy Spirit. These last two factors were naturally of first importance, but whereas the remission of sins applied equally to all (the early writers stressed this remission as a total remission for everybody: there were no little bits of sin left over), grace was received in proportion to one's faith. The greater that faith, the greater the grace received.

Just when this grace was communicated, however, was not clearly specified. Jerome (c. 345–420) had no doubt that it came with the baptismal submersion itself, and there were many who thought as he did. But over the course of time, it came to be generally accepted that whereas baptism proper washed away sin, the communication of grace was effected after the candidate had climbed out of the font, had been anointed with holy oil, and had received the laying on of hands. Since the Greek word for this holy oil is 'chrism' (it was basically pure olive oil to which a number of perfumes and spices could be added), the Greek churches refer to this rite as chrismation. The west, as we shall see in a moment, prefers the term 'confirmation'. But although the eastern and western churches differed in the emphasis they placed on the two parts of the rite (the east stressed the anointing; the west, the laying on of hands), both were quite sure that it was essential, and both insisted that it should follow immediately after submersion, just as the dove of the Holy Spirit had descended on Christ immediately after he had come up out of the waters of the Jordan.

For some three centuries, the Church restricted the administration of regular baptism to Easter or Pentecost (the feasts celebrating the Resurrection of Christ and the Descent of the Holy Spirit respectively), but recognized that in an emergency, it could be performed at any time. But with the rapid increase in the number of Christians in the wake of imperial approval in the course of the fourth century, the feast of the Epiphany (6 January) also came to be considered an appropriate time, and then, from the fifth century onwards, against some formidable opposition (by Leo the Great, for example), Christmas and other major feasts were also thought suitable. The increasing numbers of candidates affected not only the time of baptism, but the actual way in which the rite was conducted. In the earliest Church, the bishop alone took responsibility for both baptism and chrismation, but with more and more candidates appearing and more and more churches being built, it gradually became logistically impossible for him to continue this one-man practice. So what was to be done?

East and west (as usual) found different solutions. In the east, both baptism and chrismation passed into the hands of the local priest, and the bishop's role was restricted to the rite of consecrating the chrism before it was sent out to the local clergy. In modern Orthodoxy, this consecration is further restricted to bishops who are the heads of autocephalous (self-governing) churches. In the west, only the rite of baptism passed to the local priest, and the laying on of hands remained an episcopal prerogative; and since the bishop obviously could not be present at the baptism of every child, the laying on of hands tended to be delayed until there were sufficient candidates to warrant an episcopal visitation, or until the bishop had time to attend to the matter. This might be days, months, or years later, and the western idea that confirmation should be conferred at the age of reason—seven or as soon after that as was convenient—did not appear until the later Middle Ages. But the fact that there was usually a delay between baptism and confirmation demanded some investigation of precisely what happened on these two distinct occasions. If we maintain that baptism only removes sin, and that grace is not communicated until the laying on of hands, then what happens to a child in the period—possibly the very long period—between the two ceremonies? In the east, of course, this was not a problem, for chrismation followed directly on baptism (it still does), and precisely when the various effects occurred never became a question of any importance. Whatever was due to happen had certainly happened by the end of the single ceremony. But in the west this was not the case. Was the child left entirely graceless between the two rites? Or was it that grace was indeed communicated in the actual submersion (as Jerome said it was), but that the laying on of hands somehow aroused it further, or strengthened it, or *confirmed* it? It was, of course, this last solution which the west came to adopt.

The idea of 'confirming' or strengthening, however, was not a western invention. It can be traced back to Greek writers of the late second century, and in the third and fourth centuries it received a gradually increasing emphasis. The actual Latin term—*confirmatio*—first appears in a western document from the middle of the fifth century, and the theory of what happens is clearly expressed in a Latin sermon which circulated very widely in the west, and which was almost certainly written by a fifth-century cleric called Faustus (d. *c.* 490), bishop of Riez in the south of France. According to Faustus, the grace of the Holy Spirit is indeed communicated during the actual baptism, and if one were to die straightaway, that grace would be more than sufficient to ensure one's entry into the kingdom of heaven. But if one survives baptism and then goes on to live for many more years, as most of us do, additional help is necessary to fight the temptations and perils of life in this world. This is where confirmation comes in: it is the blessing of the Holy Spirit in which one is provided with the necessary spiritual weapons and the strength to use them. Or, if we may use a modern analogy, it is the booster shot which strengthens and renders fully effective a prior vaccination.

Let us turn now to the question of the age at which baptism should be administered. It is well known that most of the churches of the west and all the churches of the east baptize in infancy, and in so doing they follow a tradition which may possibly—though not certainly—be traced right back to the New Testament. Be that as it may, there is no doubt that by the end of the second century infant baptism was not uncommon, and it spread fairly widely during the course of the third century. There was always opposition to the practice, primarily from those who, like Tertullian in the west or Cyril of Jerusalem in the east, considered that conversion to Christianity was an undertaking of the utmost seriousness, and that people should not be expected to shoulder its burdens (and receive its benefits) unless they were fully cognizant of exactly what they were doing. On the other hand, there were also those—and they soon proved to be the majority—who emphasized the great desirability of having a child be a full, initiated member of the Church from as early a date as possible. If God's grace is indeed offered freely to us, should we not make sure that our children receive it at the earliest opportunity?

With the increasing numbers of babies born to Christian parents, and with the development of the doctrine of penance to deal with the problem of post-baptismal sin (we shall speak of this in a moment), infant baptism gradually became the norm, and the immense authority of Augustine in the west simply confirmed what, by his time, was effectively the standard practice. In Augustine's opinion, as we know, infants come into this world not just stained, but utterly corrupted by Adam's sin, and if they die uncleansed and unbaptized, they must therefore bear the consequences of this sin and go to hell. Their punishment may be the lightest possible punishment, that is true, but they are still condemned to some sort of eternal torment. We discussed the matter in Chapter Twelve. It was therefore considered essential, absolutely essential, for an infant to be baptized and cleansed of original sin as soon as possible, and with the triumph of Augustinianism in the west, this became standard western doctrine. Quite how it can be reconciled with the Augustinian doctrine of predestination is difficult to explain. It would seem that we are reduced to suggesting that all infants should be baptized—just in case. Those who are predestined to glory will have their sins washed away and will go to meet their Maker; those who are vessels of wrath, made for destruction, will presumably go to hell in any case, baptism or no baptism. In the opinion of many such a solution can hardly be called attractive, or, indeed, Christian.

In the east, of course, the question did not arise. The eastern churches had never accepted the Augustinian principle of total human depravity, and although the bishops at the Council of Ephesus in 431 (the Third Ecumenical Council) certainly condemned the ideas of Pelagius, they did not accept the ideas of Augustine. It is one thing to reject the principle that we have absolute freedom of choice to do good or evil; it is quite another to maintain that we are so corrupted that we cannot, of our own power, do a single good act. In the east, therefore, the defenders of infant baptism laid greater stress on the positive aspects of the rite (incorporation into the body of Christ and the reception of sanctifying grace) rather than the negative (the removal of original sin and the avoidance of hell).

On the other hand, no one denied that baptism washes away sins, and once it had become established practice to baptize children, Christians could not avoid the problem of what to do about sins committed after baptism. In the late fourth century, there appeared a small and heretical body within the Church who thought that baptism not only cleansed one from sins past, but also prevented one from sinning in the future—this could indeed be one interpretation of 1 John 3:9[1]—but the overwhelming orthodox opinion held that this was absolute rubbish, and that anyone who maintained it knew neither the Scriptures nor humankind. One solution, of course, was to defer baptism to as late a date as possible (Constantine, for instance, who had sinned more spectacularly than most men, wisely delayed his baptism until he was almost dead), but this had to be balanced against the danger of sure damnation if one failed to get to the font on time.

To deal with the problem the church developed the doctrine of penance, and there is a wealth of material on the subject from the later fourth century onwards. The Cappadocian Fathers, for example, provide copious information on the length and severity of penance, and they, with many others, sought to distinguish major sins (which certainly included apostasy, murder, and adultery) from those with less dire consequences. The schism of the Novatianists, who refused to accept that there was any forgiveness for major sins committed after baptism, also forced the orthodox to look very seriously at the matter, and not only to state, but also to defend, the contrary view. Penance came to be regarded as—and also termed—a 'second baptism', and like the first baptism, it cleansed one from all the dross and sin which one had accumulated up to the time it was undertaken. But like the first baptism, penance could only be performed once, and again like the first baptism, it was a public act. Sinners had to ask for penance from the bishop, and if this were granted, they were immediately excluded from the eucharist, and had to undergo an extremely severe course of prayer, fasting, and almsgiving for as long as the bishop thought necessary. They also had to have their hair cut short, and when they attended church, they wore a distinctive garment and worshipped in a separate part of the building. In other words, if you were a penitent, everybody knew you were a penitent.

---

1. 'No one born of God commits sin, for [God's] seed (*sperma* in Greek) remains in them, and they cannot sin because they are born of God.' Exactly how we are to translate *sperma* in this difficult verse is unclear.

For serious sins, such as incest or murder, penance could last for years, and only after this gruelling period had been completed was the cleansed sinner restored to the congregation and to communion. But even then, he or she was doomed to life-long continence, and those who were married were required to live together as brother and sister, not as man and wife. The pleasures of sexual intercourse were forbidden.

It will not come as a surprise, therefore, to learn, firstly, that this 'second baptism' was normally deferred until one's deathbed, and, secondly, that it was just too severe to last. In the late sixth century the system began to collapse, and over the ensuing decades public profession of sins became private, penances became more lenient and formal, the demand for sexual abstinence was quietly dropped, and the sacrament of forgiveness could be repeated as often as was necessary. These, however, are details outside the scope of our present study.[2]

Baptism, chrismation, and penance were undoubtedly sacraments of the first importance, yet they were still very much 'signs' of a sacred reality. The water in the font remained water; the chrism remained chrism. No change occurred in their substantial nature. But in the eucharist, this was not the case. In one sense the bread and wine were simply 'signs' or symbols of invisible grace, but in another they were true flesh and blood, and were therefore the realities themselves. We may say at the outset that this was something never denied by the Fathers or Mothers of the Church, and was never a subject of controversy. Disputes over the real presence do not occur before the ninth century,[3] and Christian writers from Ignatius of Antioch to Augustine and beyond had no difficulty in believing that when Christ said 'This is my body', that was precisely what he meant. Neither did these writers see the slightest incompatibility between viewing the bread and wine sometimes symbolically and sometimes realistically—the two viewpoints were never seen as being in any way mutually exclusive—and although we do find differences

---

2. See Bell, *Many Mansions. An Introduction to the Development and Diversity of Medieval Theology West and East* (Kalamazoo/Spencer, 1996) 315–320.

3. See *ibid.*, Chapter Fifteen.

of emphasis (the early Alexandrians, as we might expect, were the symbolists *par excellence*; the Antiochenes emphasized that there was bread and flesh, flesh and bread, two distinct realities), everyone was agreed that in the eucharistic rite a definite and undoubted change did occur. The first to state this clearly may have been Justin Martyr, but he only echoes a common idea. These early writers had no standard terminology for the eucharistic miracle—for some the bread and wine 'changed', for others they were 'converted' or 'refashioned' or 'transmuted', and neither did they have any precise theory as to how the change took place. But they had not the slightest difficulty in accepting it as an undeniable and undisputed fact of the faith that they did change.

Justin also provides us with a fascinating—though incomplete—description of just what happened at a second-century Eucharist, and much of what he says would be familiar to practising Christians today. It is true that much more of the liturgy was extemporary—the presiding elder made up the prayers as he went along—but the essential features have remained constant for almost two thousand years. A weekly eucharistic liturgy took place on Sundays, and consisted of scriptural readings, prayers, a homily, the kiss of peace, the consecration of the bread and wine, the distribution of the eucharistic gifts, and a collection to be used for all those in need, such as widows and orphans, the sick, those in prison, and strangers visiting from other areas of the early Christian world.

But Justin's description also makes it quite clear that by his time, the Eucharist was not intended to be a full-scale repast—as it seems once to have been—but rather a token meal, and that the convivial atmosphere of a dinner party had given way to the more sombre and ritualistic aspect of formal worship. The very earliest Christians seem not to have made this distinction, and their *agapē* or 'love-feast' was a re-enactment of the real and substantial meal taken by Christ with his disciples before his execution. You ate and drank to fill yourself on these occasions; you rejoiced and gave thanks, as Christ had done at the Last Supper.[4] 'Thanksgiving', in fact, is what the Greek word

4. See Mt 26:27, 1 Cor 11:24, and elsewhere.

'eucharist' means. But it is clear from the problems Paul had to face in Corinth[5] that the rejoicing could sometimes get out of hand. By the end of the first century, therefore, the ritualistic Eucharist had been distinguished from the dinner party, and the early writers were universally agreed that its weekly celebration not only symbolized most effectively the unity of the Church, but was also the most efficacious way in which this unity was actually brought about.

In baptism, as we have seen, one is 'incorporated' into the mystical body of Christ, but in the Eucharist one is joined to Christ in a yet more intimate relationship. Not only does the shared meal symbolize the unity of the body of Christ and its members, but the body of Christ actually enters the believers and is made one with them. Communicants become (in the words of Cyril of Jerusalem) 'Christ-bearers',[6] and thereby share or participate in the divine nature. By taking Christ bodily within themselves, Christians are gradually transformed into Christ, and hence into God. It follows, therefore, that the Eucharist was seen by both western and eastern writers (but especially the latter) as the most important means of human 'deification' or 'divinization'. By the gradual transformation which is effected by the body and blood of Christ, Christians in turn become more truly the mystical body of Christ, and the Church, thereby feeding on itself, becomes more truly what it actually is.

How the change from bread to body, or wine to blood, was actually brought about was not a matter of great concern to the theologians of the early Church. They believed without question that a change did occur, and, on the whole, did not care to speculate on the mechanism. The only notable exception is Gregory of Nyssa, and we should perhaps say a word about his theory—not because it is successful (one cannot, after all, explain the inexplicable), but because it is the only early theory we have. Christ, says Gregory, ate and drank, and by the usual metabolic processes, what he ate and drank was slowly transformed into his body and blood. It is therefore possible to see in this process not a change from one thing, X, to

5. See 1 Cor 7–8 and 11:20–34.
6. Cyril of Jerusalem, *Catecheses mystagogicae*, 4.3.

another thing, Y, utterly different and alien, but a transmutation of something which is *potentially* X to something which is *actually* X. Bread, for a human being, is potentially body, and wine is potentially blood, so what happens in the Eucharist is that God, by his divine power, transforms the potential into the actual, and does not perform a conjuring trick like changing a handkerchief into a rabbit. And then, Gregory continues, the real flesh and blood of Christ is taken into ourselves, and they fuse or meld or mix or blend (the Greek verb means all these things) with us, so that by sharing in Christ's immortality we, too, may become immortal.[7]

The writers of the patristic period were also quite certain that the Eucharist was a sacrifice. They qualify the term with such words as 'spiritual' sacrifice or 'bloodless' sacrifice, but they were in no doubt that when the body of Christ was offered up by the priest at the altar, it was a true re-enactment of the sacrifice at Calvary. But since there was only one Calvary, and since there are as many altars as there are churches, does this mean that there are many sacrifices and many bodies? No, said the Fathers, it does not. Since Christ has only one body, there can be only one sacrifice. We always offer the same person. We always offer the same victim. We always offer the same oblation. John Chrysostom, bishop of Constantinople at the very end of the fourth century (before he died in tragic circumstances in 407), is one of the clearest exponents of this idea, but he speaks not for himself but for all Christians. 'If the sacrifice is offered in many places', he asks, 'does this mean that there are many Christs? Of course not! Christ is everywhere one, complete in this place, complete in that, one body . . . and therefore one sacrifice.'[8] Furthermore, because there is but one sacrifice, and because that sacrifice is spiritually identical with the sacrifice on Calvary, the effects of the Calvary sacrifice are also manifested in the Eucharist. And since one of the most important effects of the crucifixion was the forgiveness of sins and the redemption of the world, so, too, in the Eucharist these effects are reenacted, represented (in the literal sense of 're-presented', 'presented once

---

7. Gregory of Nyssa, *Oratio catechetica*, 37.87.
8. John Chrysostom, *Homilia* 17 *in Hebraeos*, 3.

again'), and reapplied. The eucharistic sacrifice does not *add* to the
Calvary sacrifice—but it continually 'realizes' it: continually makes
it real and present.

On the other hand, the body of Christ is not only the bread on
the altar, but also the Church. It follows, then, as Augustine points
out, that when the Church offers up Christ in the eucharistic sacrifice, it also offers up itself. It is not only the sacrifice of Christ,
bringing with it redemption and remission of sins, but a self-sacrifice
of all those individual Christians who are the members of his body.
'The whole redeemed community,' says Augustine,

> that is, the congregation and society of the saints, is offered
> to God as a universal sacrifice through the great Priest, who
> also offered himself in his Passion for us, so that we might
> be the body of such a great head. . . This is the sacrifice of
> Christians—who are many, but one body in Christ [Rom
> 12:5]—which the church repeatedly celebrates in the sacra-
> ment of the altar, so familiar to the faithful. Here it is shown
> to [the church] that in what it offers, it is itself offered.'[9]

This is a remarkable doctrine, and there is no doubt that all these
ideas may be combined together to produce a rich and impressive
theory of the Eucharist and its effects. By participation in this rite
individual Christians assert their membership in the Church, and
are mystically united with the body and blood of their risen Lord.
By this uniting they share in the attributes of this Lord, most especially in his immortality and perfection, though the full realization
of these is reserved for the life to come. By participation in the Eucharist, Christians 'incorporate' themselves into the body of Christ,
and are themselves 'impregnated' by the body into which they are
incorporated. They become 'Christ-bearers', and the Christ within
them both demands and makes possible a more perfect and more
Christian life. At the Eucharist the historical event of Calvary—the
one sufficient sacrifice, once offered—is transformed into an ever-

---

9. Augustine of Hippo, *De civitate Dei*, 10.6.

present and ever-repeated reality, which, by its very nature, brings with it redemption and the remission of sins. And finally, in this comprehensive act, the Church sacrifices itself to the Lord who sacrificed himself for it, and since eternal life is promised only to those who have no concern for their lives in this world (Jn 12:25), the Eucharist is a pledge and guarantee of immortality.

Let us now, therefore, investigate where this immortality is to be enjoyed (or endured). What is the nature of heaven (and hell), and what dramatic events await us when we shuffle off this mortal coil and pass into that country from whose bourn no traveller returns? What is the nature of the Christian's hope and the Christian's expectation?

At the heart of the celestial city, surrounded by its towering walls, is the Trinity in an almond-shaped oval of glory called a mandorla. In the centre of the mandorla is God the Father, with the Lamb of God (symbolizing the Son) on his right, and the dove of the Holy Spirit on his left. Around the Trinity are angels, patriarchs, and the symbols of the four Evangelists: an eagle for John, an ox for Luke, a lion for Mark, and a man or angel for Matthew. Below are sixteen saints, and four figures belonging to the ecclesiastical hierarchy and the Bohemian royal family who commissioned the manuscript.

THE HEAVENLY JERUSALEM

from a twelfth-century manuscript of the De civitate Dei *of Augustine of Hippo*
Location: Archives, Hradcany Castle, Prague, Czech Republic
Photo: Erich Lessing/Art Resource, New York

XVI

LAST THINGS

IT SEEMS FITTING, if predictable, that we should devote this last chapter to a discussion of the last things: those momentous events which will bring this world to its close and ourselves to judgement. The writers of the early Church were quite certain that three events would be involved: the Second Coming of Christ; a General Resurrection; and a Last Judgement, after which we would be justly consigned either to eternal bliss or eternal torment. On the other hand, these same writers were also convinced that in our efforts to gain the joys of heaven and avoid the pains of hell we were neither alone nor unaided. There were those who had run the race before us, who had achieved the goal, and who—if we would only ask—were

ready and eager to intercede for us with the Almighty and to seek
to mitigate what, for us sinners, would be only too just a judgement.
We are here speaking of the saints and devotion to the saints, and
there is no doubt that both played an increasingly important role in
the theology and practice of the early Church.

The early Fathers found support for the idea in Christ's promise
to his apostles that, in the world to come, they would sit on twelve
thrones judging the twelve tribes of Israel (Mt 19: 28). In other
words, that there were some who would enjoy special privileges
in the next world, and that they would have some say in the matter of judgement. They also knew that, in the parable of Dives and
Lazarus, the rich man asked the patriarch Abraham to send Lazarus
to his—the rich man's—brothers so that they might be warned and
escape the torments of hell (Lk 16:27-28). This, thought the early
Fathers, was clear and incontrovertible evidence that the dead could
intercede for the living, though in this particular case, it seems not
to have done much good.

Furthermore, the whole Pauline concept of the Mystical Body
of Christ implied a continuity between this world and the next, between the living and the dead. We are all, individually, 'members one
of another' (Rom 12:5), 'fellow-citizens of the saints and members of
God's household' (Eph 2:19), and if Christ himself is eternal, being
bound neither by space nor by time, so, too, is his Mystical Body. It
follows, therefore, that the members of this body exist in a mystical
communion, a spiritual unity; and if the dead can intercede for the living, so, too, the living may intercede for the dead. That this was done,
and done from an early date, is not in question. Many inscriptions
in the catacombs, dating back to the second century, contain prayers
for the repose and well-being of those who have died. Tertullian tells
us plainly that it was a regular practice, though he admits that it does
not have explicit scriptural authority. It is part of the faith, he says,
and has its origins in tradition and is confirmed by custom.[1]

If, then, the dead may indeed intercede for the living, with whom
do they intercede? The answer, ultimately, must be God, for only God

---

1. Tertullian, *De corona militis*, 4.1.

can forgive sins and intervene in the process of judicial sentencing. And who is God most likely to listen to? To those, obviously, who deserve a hearing, those who, by their courage, devotion, piety, and zeal, have shown themselves to be his true and loving servants. And who are they? The Church of the second and third centuries was not in doubt: it was the martyrs. They, above all, had kept the faith. They had paid the ultimate price, often in circumstances of hideous torment. They had died for their Lord, as their Lord had died for them. It is surely only reasonable to expect that God would hear their pleas and bend a willing ear to their requests.

Communication with the martyr-saints was made easier because of their relics. These provided material and worldly contact-points with immaterial and heavenly intercessors, and they acted in much the same way as a modern cordless telephone with just a single number in the memory. They were of the utmost importance. Thus, in the moving account of the martyrdom of Polycarp, the aged bishop of Smyrna (he was eighty-six when he was burned), probably written in about 156, we are told how his followers were eager to claim their share of what was left of his body. His bones, they said, 'are more precious to us than gems, and more valuable than gold'; and after they had collected them together, they buried them in a suitable location. For reasons of security, they do not name the place, but wherever it was, 'it is there that we shall gather in joy and gladness, and, with the Lord's permission, celebrate the birthday of his martyrdom'.[2] This is the earliest record we have of a practice which would later become standard, that of celebrating a saint's 'birthday' on the day of his or her death.

Not all who were tortured died. In Chapter Four, for example, we saw how Origen survived the tortures inflicted upon him during the Decian persecution, and there were many others like him. But there was no doubt that they, too, had borne witness to the faith by their sufferings, and that after their deaths (often hastened by their torments), they, too, might intercede for us with God. Cyprian of Carthage tells us so quite plainly. Such men and women were

2. *Martyrdom of Polycarp*, 17–18.

therefore referred to as 'witnesses', or, in Latin, *confessores*, 'confessors'. The Latin verb from which the title derives means, in this instance, 'to bear witness'.

The period of persecution came to an end with the Edict of Toleration in 311 and the Edict of Milan in 313.[3] As a consequence, the possibility of dying or suffering for the faith was seriously curtailed. Yet, from this time onwards, devotion to the saints became ever more popular, and the number of those recognized for their holiness increased dramatically. The reason was simple. The Church soon came to accept that a life of holiness, asceticism, austerity, and renunciation might equal the devotion of those who had actually suffered and died for Christ. Indeed, even a life wholly dedicated to the service of God or of the Church (they were regarded, unwisely, as essentially the same thing) might be seen as a just equivalent to the torments of martyrdom, and even the display of what, in later centuries, would come to be known as 'heroic virtue' might be regarded as a sufficient claim to sanctity. It is not surprising, therefore, that men such as Athanasius the Great and John Chrysostom soon came to be venerated as saints by the eastern Church, as also did many ascetics, both male and female; and in the west, at Carthage, Augustine was venerated as a saint before 475, less than fifty years after his death.

We should note, however, that at this time there was no universal, formal rite of canonization, either in the west or the east. Nor were there any clearly defined criteria for elevation to sanctity. Apart from the martyrs and confessors, certain major figures, as we have mentioned, soon came to be regarded as effective intercessors, and many local churches venerated local saints, some very local indeed. In the west, in later centuries, it came to be accepted that only the pope could declare a person a saint, and the first formal canonization to be historically attested is that of Ulrich of Augsburg (*c.* 890–973), who, apart from being a major player in the ecclesiastical politics of his time, was also an effective bishop with high moral sensibilities. He was canonized by Pope John XV at the end of January 993, though

---

3. See Chapter One.

it cannot be denied that his canonization was, to a large extent, politically motivated. In the Orthodox east, canonization came usually to be conferred by a synod of bishops of a self-governing Church, though this is not always the case. To pursue this matter further, however, would take us well into the Middle Ages and beyond, and that is too far from our present course.

Suffice it to say that we are not unaided in our quest for Paradise, and that Christians from the second century onwards were convinced that the martyrs, confessors, and saints, both male and female, were eager and willing to intercede for them with God, and thereby bring about a mitigation of what, if justice were to be strictly applied, might be an extraordinarily unpleasant period in eternity. In the west, of course, the Reformation of the sixteenth century would bring about major changes. All this brings us back to the question of the Last Things.

As we said at the beginning of this chapter, the writers of the early Church were all alike convinced that at the end of time Christ would come again, and that there would then follow a General Resurrection and Last Judgement. But beyond an almost universal acceptance of these three factors, there was considerable disagreement as to where, when, and how these cataclysmic events would take place. Three questions in particular demanded their attention. First, was there to be an interval between the Second Coming and the General Resurrection, and if so, how long was it to last? Secondly, what happened to individual souls in the period between the death of the body and the General Resurrection? And thirdly, what sort of body was it that arose at the sound of the Last Trump? Let us begin with the first question.

The twentieth chapter of the Book of Revelation is full of the idea of a thousand-year reign. Satan is bound for a thousand years; the martyrs reign with Christ for a thousand years; there is a cataclysm at the end of the thousand years. These ideas came over into Christianity from the messianic speculations of later Judaism, and they proved very popular during the first two centuries. Jesus would descend to earth—almost certainly in Jerusalem—and would then establish an earthly kingdom which would last for a millennium. It would be a time of peace and plenty. The righteous would rise from the dead to enjoy it, and if we may believe Irenaeus of Lyons, food of every kind would be available in overwhelming abundance. Every grain of wheat, he tells us, will produce ten thousand ears; every ear will produce ten thousand grains; and every grain will produce ten pounds of the finest flour. (If these are Roman pounds, by the way, this gives us nearly three hundred and thirty-five thousand tons of flour per grain of wheat: the righteous saints must have been over-whelmed.) All the animals will live in peace and harmony (an idea borrowed from Isaiah 11; even lions turn vegetarian), and all nature will be totally obedient.[4] Certain heretical groups (like the followers of Cerinthus, a Gnostic teacher who flourished at the end of the first century) went further than this, and envisaged the millennium as a thousand years of indulgence in gluttony, lechery, drinking parties, and banquets. But this was not, emphatically not, the teaching of the 'official' Christian Church.

These millennial ideas were widespread and popular, but despite the authority of such formidable figures as Irenaeus, Justin, Hip-polytus, and Tertullian, Origen was not prepared to accept them. As a true Alexandrian his approach was naturally much more allegorical, and he reinterpreted both the Second Coming and the millennium in a fully spiritual sense. He was well aware of the arguments in use and the proof-texts cited, and he knew that there were many who believed that the righteous saints would eat and drink and copulate in the New Jerusalem. But though these people believe in Christ, he says, they are interpreting the divine Scriptures in a Jewish way, and that is not fitting for Christians. Yes, the saints will eat, but what they will eat will be the bread of life which feeds the soul and il-luminates the mind with the food of wisdom and truth. Yes, they will drink, but what they will drink will come from the cup of divine wisdom. And this food and drink will serve not to feed the body and satisfy the senses, but to restore the soul to the image and likeness of God.[5]

---

4. Irenaeus of Lyons, *Adversus Haereses*, V, xxxiii, 3–4.

5. This and the material at n. 11 below is synthesized from a number of Origen's writings.

The arguments of Origen were certainly persuasive, and they came at a time when there was a general and growing dissatisfaction with more physical and materialistic interpretations of Christ's Second Coming; and although belief in the millennium lingered on in some places for a further century, it did so only as the view of a small and uninfluential minority. By Origen's time, the majority view was that the General Resurrection would follow directly upon the Second Coming, and this naturally introduces the question of just what happens to an individual's soul immediately after physical death. Is it conscious or unconscious? Is it aware or unaware? Where does it go? Is it judged at that time as well as at the General Resurrection?

The Gnostics, on the whole, maintained that once the soul is released from the body by death, it immediately begins its ascent to heaven. In natural opposition to this thesis, the anti-Gnostic writers—Irenaeus, for example—asserted the contrary. As Christ descended into hell for three days, so the souls of the departed enter an invisible underworld, 'the shadow of death', marked out for them by God. There they must wait until the Resurrection, when they will receive back their bodies, and arise, whole and complete, to be ushered into the presence of their Creator.[6] Tertullian is even more explicit. For him, the underworld is a vast emptiness or a concealed abyss deep in the earth, and it is here that the souls of the dead await the Resurrection. So long as the earth remains intact, therefore, there is no way out of this deep pit, and only when the earth is shattered at the end of all things will the souls there imprisoned be released. But, says Tertullian, in this underworld there is both punishment and refreshment: a sort of anticipation of the eternal bliss or eternal torment yet to come. It would be unjust, he says, if in that dark cavern the souls of the wicked prospered, or the souls of the righteous were afflicted. So if we interpret 'the last penny' of Matthew 5:26 correctly, we find that it refers to 'every trifling transgression which must be expiated there in the period before the Resurrection'.[7] This is clearly an anticipation of the later doctrine of purgatory. Tertullian

6. *Ibid.*, V.xxxi.2.
7. Tertullian, *De anima*, 58.

does not here mention fire, true, and in another of his writings he seems to indicate that these little sins must be expiated during our life here and not hereafter, but despite his uncertainties, there is no doubt that he is beginning to think in purgatorial terms.

Clement of Alexandria carries the idea further, and maintains, more specifically, that if people repent on their death-beds and therefore have no opportunity of performing penance here and now, they may be cleansed in the next life by purifying fire. There are some, he says, like the deaf adders of Psalm 58:4, who will not listen to the Lord's song. Let them be chastised, therefore, by God's fatherly admonitions *before* the final judgement, so that by being ashamed and repenting, they may not inherit eternal pain. Most of us, Clement continues, have deserved these chastisements, but even though we have fallen into sin, we are still of the Lord's people.[8]

Nevertheless, despite the evidence that such ideas were in circulation, it would be premature to speak of a 'doctrine' of purgatory. There was just too much uncertainty surrounding the question of what happened to the soul immediately after death—particularly among the eastern theologians—and although in the west the ideas rapidly coalesced, it is not until after the time of Augustine that we can begin to speak of a doctrine of purgatory with any real meaning. But from the third century onwards, it seems that the Christian consensus was that after death, the soul was not in a state of sleep, unconsciousness, or suspended animation. On the contrary. It awaited the final judgement with its senses intact, and it probably (though not certainly) anticipated that judgement with either pain or happiness. The pain then served to cleanse the soul of at least minor sins, so that by the time of the judgement itself it could appear before its Creator in as clean a condition as possible. Not until Jerome is this immediate foretaste referred to specifically as a 'judgement', and not until the fourteenth century do we find it officially recognized as part of the doctrine of the Church. At that time Pope Benedict XII (1334–1342) denied any intermediate post-mortem state in which the souls of the departed 'anticipated' the future consequences of

8. Clement of Alexandria, *Stromateis*, VII.16 (102).

their earthly actions. Instead, he declared, there was an immediate judgement, and the souls of the dead went straightaway to heaven, hell, or purgatory.[9] But even with papal authority behind it, there was still considerable medieval uncertainty over the matter, and the situation a thousand years earlier was much more fluid.

In any case, the biblical evidence itself is conflicting. Whereas some texts indicate without question that the General Resurrection, Second Coming, and Final Judgement were intimately related, the parable of Dives and Lazarus seemed to some to imply that there is an immediate and particular judgement following bodily death. Confusion and uncertainty were only to be expected, therefore, and although the idea of what we might call 'anticipated judgement' (which might or might not be purgatorial) was certainly widespread, it would be quite incorrect to refer to it as a 'doctrine' of the Church. It was, however, the most widely circulated idea among a considerable number of other ideas and speculations.

Despite the general acceptance of some sort of 'anticipated judgement', none of the early writers ever denied the Final Judgement yet to come. Nor did they deny, as a prelude to that awesome event, the resurrection of the body. But what sort of body? The physical one we have now, with all its cuts, bruises, pimples, and hæmorrhoids? Or a spiritual body (as Saint Paul suggests in 1 Cor 15:44) in which all these things are transformed and transcended?

The earliest writers—the Apostolic Fathers and the Apologists— tended to the first of these two alternatives. Given the problems they had with Gnosticism, this is understandable, for the Gnostics (as we saw in Chapter Two) considered matter, flesh, and created stuff to be evil, and they utterly denied the possibility of solid flesh inhabiting the wholly transcendent kingdom of the Supreme Being. For them, resurrection was entirely spiritual, the body was thankfully left behind to rot away in the earth, and the earth was welcome to it.

9. See David N. Bell, *Many Mansions. An Introduction to the Development and Diversity of Medieval Theology West and East* (Kalamazoo–Spencer, 1996) 342–343.

No, said the Christians, this is not the case at all. The resurrection of Christ anticipates our resurrection, and in the ascension of Christ, it was not just his soul that ascended into heaven, but his soul in its resurrected body. In any case, they said, God can do anything, and if he could make a human body with all its muscles and veins and bones and blood and life and rationality (this is Irenaeus of Lyons speaking), he would surely have no problem resurrecting this same body once it had returned to its constituent elements. Look at the seasons, says Tertullian: winter follows autumn, autumn follows summer, summer follows spring. The trees bare their branches and are reclothed in green; the flowers look dead, but then burst forth in glory! They all return after they have departed; they all begin again after they have faded away. 'Nothing perishes except to be restored, and the whole order of things . . . is a witness to the resurrection of the dead.'[10] In any case, if your flesh with all its idiosyncrasies does not rise, how can you be sure that God will recognize you? I may have no objection to being accredited, by error, with other people's merits, but I have no desire to be mistakenly saddled with their sins.

To this literal and materialistic interpretation of resurrection, the allegorical Origen strongly objected. This, by now, should cause us no surprise. He does not, of course, deny the doctrine—to do so would be to deny a fundamental principle of the Christian tradition—but he reinterprets it in what is, for him, a more satisfactory sense. What he says, effectively, is that all bodies are in a state of metabolic transformation, and that during the course of one's life the actual bodily stuff of which one is made is in a state of unceasing change. Yet despite this, an individual of twenty is, in a certain way, the same individual at sixty, and can be recognized as such. This is because there is a bodily 'form' or 'shape' or 'appearance' which remains essentially constant while all else changes. It is like the river of Heraclitus: the water in which I am paddling now is not the same water as it was ten seconds ago. To that extent it is a totally different river. Yet I still recognize it as the same stream. So when the saints

10. Tertullian, *De resurrectione carnis*, 12.

rise again, says Origen, they will retain the same form/shape/appearance, but the substances which make up this form will not be the fleshly ones, suitable for fleshly life on this earth, but spiritual ones, suitable for spiritual life in heaven. 'It is sown in corruption; it is raised in incorruption. It is sown in dishonour; it is raised in glory. It is sown in weakness; it is raised in power. It is sown an animal body; it is raised a spiritual body' (1 Cor 15:42-44).[11]

This transformational concept may, on the whole, be more satisfactory for many modern Christian believers, but it was certainly not a concept which went unchallenged. Some opponents pointed out that the physical form or appearance is the least constant thing about the body, and it is certainly the thing that perishes first when death and decay and worms take over. Others pointed to Christ's meeting with doubting Thomas. If that disciple could actually put his fingers in the holes left by the nails and the spear, then it must have been the same flesh that died on the cross. Transfigured, perhaps, and transformed and spiritualized and resurrected, but basically and substantially the same flesh.

Such objections were not without force. If I make a statue of a person out of silver, melt it down, and then make a second statue of the same person out of gold, can we really call it the same statue? What Origen's opponents wanted to do was to replace the idea of *substitution* (substituting spiritual matter for fleshly matter) with *spiritualization* or *transformation*. Here we make our statue from lead, and then God the Divine Alchemist, in ways known only to himself, *transforms* or *spiritualizes* the lead into gold. It is indeed the fleshly body which is raised, but by God's spiritualizing influence the resurrected flesh has certain properties which it does not at present possess. It will be immortal, for example, and no longer subject to corruption. If this were not so, how could the blessed enjoy God forever or the wicked burn eternally? The act of cremation is over in a comparatively short time, and if we do not have flesh which is eternally flammable, then we would be forced to resort to a punishment similar to that found in the Qur'ān: when one lot of skin

11. See n. 5 above.

has been burned away, God creates another so that the process may continue *ad infinitum* (Qur'ān 4:56).

Hard-line Origenists were therefore few—only Gregory of Nyssa really followed closely in his master's footsteps—and the general tendency in both east and west was to adapt the 'spiritualization' rather than the 'substitution' theory. Yet the west, typically, laid greater stress than did the east on the essential identity of the physical flesh with the resurrected flesh. Jerome, reacting against Origen, is particularly insistent on this, and Augustine stresses that when Saint Paul speaks of a 'spiritual' body, he does not mean that the flesh has been converted into spirit, but that the resurrected body will submit to the spirit 'with the greatest and most wonderful ease of obedience'.[12] Yet he also admits that the new body will be incorruptible and immortal, and not only will it *not* be as it is now, even when in perfect health, it will not even be as it was in the first humans before sin. It will, instead, be better than both, and when Augustine denies the straightforward conversion of flesh into spirit, he is not denying a certain spiritualization of the fleshly elements.

For both east and west, then, the Second Coming heralded the resurrection of both good and bad, their appearance before the divine Judge in spiritualized fleshly bodies, and their ultimate consignation to heaven or to hell. But what are these places like? What are their essential characteristics? What is the nature of the infernal torments or the inconceivable joys of Paradise?

Hell and its pains are fairly well described in the New Testament, though for gory imagination and sadistic ingenuity, the biblical accounts cannot compare with the descriptions of later medieval writers. According to the Scriptures, hell is a place of outer darkness, of weeping and gnashing of teeth, of ever-burning fire (with or without brimstone), and of the worm that dieth not. It is also unquestionably everlasting, and the few brave souls who questioned this repellent doctrine had no significant impact on the orthodox Christian tradition. For Origen, for example (so frequently the odd man out), the idea of eternal torment was incompatible with the doctrine of

---

12. Augustine of Hippo, *De civitate Dei*, 13.20.

a loving God who was perfectly good, incompatible with the all-important concept of human free will, and incompatible with the Pauline statement that God will reign until he has put all his enemies under his feet (1 Cor 15:25). His view, therefore, was that after inconceivable cycles of time, all beings would achieve redemption, including Satan (the 'last enemy' of 1 Cor 15:26), and this optimistic doctrine was also the view of Origen's admirer, Gregory of Nyssa. It was not, however, the view of the other 99.99% of the Christian community, and despite occasional and momentary doubts from such stalwart guardians of orthodoxy as Gregory of Nazianzus, the universal Christian opinion by the end of the fourth century was that the torment was as eternal as it was terrible.

It was also the opinion of the Fathers that the infernal pains were physical, not psychological. Origen, inevitably, held the latter view, but hardly anyone else did. There were different degrees of torment corresponding to different degrees of sin, but whatever the degree of the torment, it was an external pain applied to bodily limbs. The fire was real, material, hot, and everlasting, and the only mitigation of this idea appears in the distinct though as-yet-unformed ideas of purgatory we discussed above. This is particularly evident in western writers, and we find such notable authorities as Ambrose of Milan and Jerome proposing that, while those totally wicked will be tormented forever, 'Christian' sinners—those who have believed in Christ, but have erred and strayed in comparatively minor ways—will be purified by the fire and eventually saved. But as we said earlier, the western doctrine of purgatory was not formalized until after the time of Augustine, and the eastern Churches—for reasons which we cannot discuss here—were eventually to reject it altogether.

What, then, of heaven? Much of the physical imagery we hear in poetry and see in pictures stems, of course, from the Book of Revelation. It is there that we find the New Jerusalem with its pearly gates (twelve of them), its streets of transparent gold, its towering walls (some 220 feet high), its square city plan (covering about two million square miles by my reckoning), the throne of God, the river, the tree of life, the crystal sea, the elders with their harps, and so on. But although these images may have been—and still are—much caressed at the popular level, many of the early writers held more refined ideas. The Alexandrian tradition, understandably, tended to think of heaven as the realm of the Platonic Ideas, of the perfect archetypes of the imperfect realities here below, to which was added the sublime vision or indescribable experience of the All-Holy Trinity itself.

This experience is the Beatific Vision, the culmination of Christian endeavour, and for the eastern Fathers it coincided with the completion of the process of deification. Gregory of Nyssa is particularly insistent on this point, and tells us that we will participate not only in the divine immortality and incorruption, but in the divine perfection and glory as well.[13] Our knowledge, so limited and fragmentary here below, is there expanded into God, and we shall contemplate and experience the vision of God, not through a glass darkly, in a riddle and an enigma, but face to face. Heaven is a realm of supreme delight and supreme rest, of unsullied joy and uttermost bliss, of meetings with loved ones past, and—as the western writers especially stressed—with the confessors and martyrs and saints whom we met at the beginning of this chapter. But just as in hell, so, too, in heaven, there are gradations, and some writers, though by no means all, suggested that even after living holy lives here on earth, the souls of the righteous in Paradise continue to make progress, stage by stage, until they achieve final beatitude. These are the 'many mansions' of which Christ spoke in the Gospel of John (Jn 14:2), but the very end of our progress (says Augustine) is the happy realization that there is indeed no end. God is Insatiable Satiety (Augustine's expression), and anyone who sinks down into that trinitarian abyss goes on sinking further down forever.

These are not concepts we can at present comprehend. The eyes and the mind of the resurrection body are subtly spiritualized, says Augustine again, and are thereby enabled to see and conceive things wholly impossible for us now. The Beatific Vision is the supreme experience, the truest and fullest happiness ever to be attained, the realization of all our desires, and the culmination of the Christian

---

13. Gregory of Nyssa, *De anima et resurrectione*.

hope. It is the endless Sabbath whose end (says Augustine, one last and final time)

> will not be an evening, but the Day of the Lord, a sort of eighth and eternal day, consecrated by the resurrection of Christ and prefiguring not only the eternal rest of the spirit, but that of the body as well. There we shall be still and we shall see; we shall see and we shall love; we shall love and we shall give praise. Behold what will be at the end without end! For what else is our end, but to attain the Kingdom which has no end?[14]

14. Augustine, *De civitate Dei*, 22.30.5.

INDEX